Table of Contents

P9-AOI-938

Acknowledgements

A Special Thanks to the following HealthforAll Staff:

Amber Slichta

Kathy Leonard

Jeannine Monteleone

Christine Osborne

Nicole Vargovich

Kate Waddington

All others who graciously donated their time:

Mary Aronica

Canisius College Marketing Department

Bridgette Cassety

Beverly Slichta-Cusick

Tom Cusick

Dog Eat Dog Advertising, Inc.

Sherry Fleckenstein

Tony Hoffman

Denise Rizzo

Stacey Slichta

Gary Wolfe

Measurement Equivalents

Liquid Measures

1 cup .... 8 fluid ounces .... ½ pint .... 237 ml .... 16 tablespoons
2 cups.................. 16 fluid ounces ..... 1 pint .... 473 ml
4 cups.................. 32 fluid ounces ..... 1 quart .... 946 ml
2 pints .... 32 fluid ounces ..... 1 quart .... 0.946 liters
4 quarts .... 128 fluid ounces ... 1 gallon .... 3.785 liters
8 quarts .... 1 peck
4 pecks .... 1 bushel
dash .... less than ¼ teaspoon
1 teaspoon .... ⅙ fluid ounce .... 5 grams .... about 5 ml
1 tablespoon .... ½ fluid ounce .... 15 grams............... 15 ml .... 3 teaspoons
2 tablespoons ...... 1 fluid ounce .... 30 grams............... 29.6 ml .... ⅛ cup
8 tablespoons ...... 4 fluid ounces .... ¼ pint .... 118.5 ml .... ½ cup

Dry Measures

3 teaspoons .... 1 tablespoon .... ½ ounce................ 14.3 grams
2 tablespoons ...... ⅛ cup .... 1 fluid ounce .... 28.35 grams
4 tablespoons ...... ¼ cup .... 2 fluid ounces .... 56.7 grams
5⅓ tablespoons ... ⅓ cup .... 2.6 fluid ounces .... 75.6 grams
8 tablespoons ...... ½ cup .... 4 ounces .... 113.4 grams ..... 1 stick butter
12 tablespoons .... ¾ cup .... 6 ounces .... .375 pound ...... 170 grams
32 tablespoons .... 2 cups .... 16 ounces .... 1 pound .... 453.6 grams
64 tablespoons .... 4 cups .... 32 ounces .... 2 pounds .... 907 grams

How To Measure

THE EQUIPMENT:

Graduated Measuring Cups
Measuring cups that resemble small pots. They are usually made of plastic or metal and come in sets of four (1 cup, ½ cup, ⅓ cup, and ¼ cup). They are excellent for measuring dry ingredients because they can easily be leveled off.

Liquid Measuring Cups
Measuring cups that look like little pitchers. They are available in 1, 2, 4, and 8-cup measures. They are generally available in plastic or glass, with the amounts indicated in cups, ounces, and milliliters.

Measuring Spoons
Come in sets of four (1 tablespoon, 1 teaspoon, ½ teaspoon, and ¼ teaspoon).

INGREDIENTS:

Butter
Each ¼ pound stick of butter or margarine measures ½ cup or 8 tablespoons. In the United States the wrapping usually has tablespoons and teaspoons marked. One stick equals ½ cup. If it has not been packed that way, pack butter or margarine into measuring spoon or measuring cup.

Sugar
Most sugar can be measured in a graduated measuring cup. Simply spoon it in and level off with the straight edge of a knife. Most recipes call for certain amounts of packed brown sugar. To measure the brown sugar, pack sugar down lightly with the back of a spoon, and level off.

Flour
In most recipes, flour is to be measured straight from the canister or package (the flour needs to be airy, if it is compact, stir it in the container before measuring). Never pack flour down into the measuring cup or tap excessively. Lightly spoon flour into graduated measuring cup, and level off with straight edge of knife. It is especially important to measure flour correctly in low-fat bread making because when we reduce the fat we do not want to dramatically increase the flour.

Summer

Summer

Cauliflower Hors D'oeuvres Appetizer

8   cups (about 3 pounds) cauliflower florets

½   cup egg substitute

2   tablespoons butter or stick margarine, melted

2   teaspoons Worcestershire sauce

1   teaspoon ground mustard

1   cup seasoned bread crumbs

⅓   cup grated Parmesan cheese

¼   teaspoon dried basil

⅛   teaspoon salt

⅛   teaspoon pepper

⅛   teaspoon paprika

     Meatless spaghetti sauce, warmed, optional

Preheat oven to 350 degrees.

Place 1-inch of water and cauliflower in saucepan; bring to a boil. Reduce heat; cover and simmer for 5 minutes. Drain and immediately place cauliflower in ice water. Drain and pat dry.

In a small bowl, combine egg substitute, butter, Worcestershire sauce and mustard. In another bowl, combine bread crumbs, Parmesan cheese, basil, salt, pepper and paprika. Dip cauliflower into the egg mixture, then coat with the crumb mixture. Place into ungreased 15 x 10 x 1-inch baking pan. Bake for 30-35 minutes or until golden. Serve with spaghetti sauce for dipping if desired.

Yield: 14 servings

ACTIVITY – The Buffalo Naval and Military Park, Buffalo (Erie) – self-guided tours through war ships and military equipment. Youth programs include overnight stays, special event planning available for private or office parties.

Avocado Dip

1	(16-ounce) can refried beans
2	avocados
1	cup mayonnaise
1	cup sour cream
½	(1-ounce) package taco seasoning mix
3	cups shredded Cheddar cheese
½	cup shredded lettuce
1	large chopped fresh tomato
2	green onions, chopped
½	cup bell pepper
¼	cup sliced black olives

Spread refried beans evenly on a medium-sized serving platter. If the beans are watery, chill for 20-30 minutes.

Peel the avocados and remove the pits. In a food processor, blend the avocados with the mayonnaise, sour cream and taco seasoning until smooth. Pour over the refried beans. Top with Cheddar cheese. Add lettuce, tomatoes, green onions, green pepper and black olives if desired. Refrigerate until serving. Serve with your favorite tortilla chips.

Yield: 16 servings

FUN FACT – Mayonnaise is said to be the invention of the French chef of the Duke de Richelieu in 1756. While the Duke was defeating the British at Port Mahon, his chef was creating a victory feast that included a sauce made of cream and eggs. When the chef realized that there was not cream in the kitchen, he improvised, substituting olive oil for the cream. A new culinary masterpiece was born, and the chef named it "Mayonnaise" in honor of the Duke's victory.

Cheesy Onion Roll-Ups

1	cup sour cream
1	(8-ounce) package cream cheese, softened
½	cup shredded Cheddar cheese
¾	cup sliced green onions
1	tablespoon lime juice
1	tablespoon seeded and minced jalapeño peppers
10	(6-inch) flour tortillas
1	(16-ounce) jar picante sauce

In a medium bowl, mix sour cream, cream cheese, Cheddar cheese, green onions, lime juice and jalapeño peppers.

Spread one side of each tortilla with the sour cream mixture. Tightly roll each tortilla. Place rolled tortillas on a medium serving dish and cover with plastic wrap. Chill in the refrigerator at least 1 hour.

Slice tortillas into 1-inch pieces. Serve with picante sauce.

Yield: 5 dozen (30 servings)

ACTIVITY – Amherst Museum, Amherst (Erie) – Eleven authentic buildings - homes, school houses, churches, barber shop from the area have been relocated, restored and furnished to depict life from the 1800's. The museum also features guided tours, artifacts, seminars, and festivals.

Fresh Fruit Dips

Marshmallow Cream Cheese Dip

1   (7-ounce) jar marshmallow fluff
1   (8-ounce) package cream cheese
1   tablespoon of orange juice or
        package of any fruit flavored
        gelatin

In a large bowl with an electric mixer combine marshmallow fluff, cream cheese and juice or gelatin until creamy.

Transfer to serving bowl and serve immediately or refrigerate, covered, for up to 1 day before serving.

Yogurt Whipped Cream Dip

1   (6 to 8-ounce) container any fruit
        flavored yogurt
1   (8-ounce) container whipped
        topping

In medium mixing bowl combine whipped topping and yogurt with a wooden spoon until thoroughly mixed.

Transfer to serving bowl and serve immediately or refrigerate, covered, for up to 1 day before serving.

Creamy Mascarpone Cheese Dip

1   (8-ounce) container mascarpone
        cheese
1   tablespoon honey
2   tablespoons chopped walnuts

In medium mixing bowl combine cheese, honey and walnuts with a wooden spoon until thoroughly mixed.

Transfer to serving bowl and serve immediately or refrigerate, covered, for up to 1 day before serving.

FUN FACT – To make perfect whipped cream, you should always start with a chilled bowl and chilled beaters.

Mozzarella "S'mores"

16   sun-dried tomato halves*

2-3   tablespoons extra-virgin olive oil,
      if needed

1   ball of fresh mozzarella
      (8 to 10-ounces), cut into
      16 pieces (cut the cheese into
      4 thick slices, then cut each
      slice into quarters), or
      16 bocconcini (bite-sized
      mozzarella balls)

16   fresh basil leaves

16   garlic rubbed grilled bread slices
      or 32 crackers

2-6   long barbecue forks or skewers

Place the tomatoes in an attractive serving bowl.

Arrange the mozzarella, basil leaves, and grilled bread or crackers in bowls or on a platter.

Set up the grill for direct grilling and preheat to high. In the best of all worlds, you'd use a charcoal grill, raking the embers into a pile at the bottom of the grill and leaving off the grill grate. If using a gas grill, preheat it super hot.

Skewer a cube of mozzarella. Roast it over the fire, turning the skewer to evenly melt the cheese. If using a gas grill, you'll need to bring it as close as possible to the fire without touching the grate. When the mozzarella begins to melt and brown, after 1-2 minutes over charcoal, a little longer over gas, use a knife or fork to scrape the cheese off the skewer onto a piece of grilled bread. Top the cheese with a basil leaf and a piece of sun-dried tomato and place a second piece of grilled bread on top. Eat at once.

Sun-dried tomatoes come in two forms: oil-packed and dried. Oil-packed tomatoes just need to be drained before you use them. The dried kind need to be soaked in water and marinated in olive oil. To reconstitute the tomatoes, place them in a heatproof bowl and add boiling water to cover. Let soak for 1 hour. Drain the tomatoes well and blot dry. Toss with the olive oil.

ACTIVITY – Buffalo Theater District, Buffalo (Erie) – Broadway musicals, innovative productions, Irish and international Classics, film series, drama, concerts and family programming entertain all ages and interests.

11

Tropical Fruit Salsa

1	cup finely diced peeled firm-ripe papaya
½	cup finely diced peeled firm-ripe mango
⅓	cup finely chopped white onion
3	tablespoons chopped fresh cilantro
1	tablespoon fresh orange juice
1	tablespoon fresh lime juice
½-1	teaspoon minced fresh jalapeño chili, including seeds
½	teaspoon salt

In large mixing bowl stir together all ingredients.

Yield: 2 cups

FITNESS FACT – Eating a lot of vegetables and many types of fruits helps to decrease the appetite. The fiber content takes up space in the stomach which produces a full feeling.

Sesame Sticks

1 ½   tablespoons butter, melted
      salt and pepper to taste
3   slices of homemade-type white
       bread, crusts discarded and
       the bread cut into ½-inch-wide
       sticks
½   cup sesame seeds

Preheat oven to 350 degrees.

Season the butter with salt and pepper. Brush it on the bread sticks. Roll the sticks in the sesame seeds.

Bake sesame sticks 15 minutes on cookie sheet in middle of the oven or until golden.

ACTIVITY – The Maid of the Mist Boat Tours, Niagara Falls (Niagara) – takes visitors to the very edge of the area where the huge torrent of Niagara Falls plunges into the Niagara River.

Broiled Shrimp Appetizer

20 large shrimp
1 cup olive oil
  Juice of 3 lemons
¼ cup soy sauce
¼ cup finely chopped parsley
3 tablespoons of fresh or dried
    tarragon

With sharp scissors cut down the back of each shrimp shell and remove the black vein but do not remove the shell. Wash the shrimp thoroughly and place them in a large bowl. Over them pour olive oil, the lemon juice, soy sauce, parsley and tarragon. Let the shrimp stand in this mixture for 2 hours, tossing them around now and then so that they will be equally marinated.

When you are ready to cook them, arrange then in basket grills and cook over hot coals for 5-6 minutes, turning twice. They should be tender and moist with lightly charred shells. Have finger bowls and pass plenty of paper napkins.

Yield: 5 servings

FUN FACT – Curly or Flat Leaf Parsley have a faint peppery tang; clean refreshing aftertaste; good companion to other fresh herbs. Use in all dishes or as a garnish. Flat leaf, also called Italian parsley, is sweeter and more flavorful than curly.

Samosas

1 cup minus 1 tablespoon all-purpose flour, divided
1 teaspoon granulated sugar
½ teaspoon salt
¼ teaspoon paprika
2 tablespoons plus 2 teaspoons margarine, chilled and cut up
3 tablespoons low-fat cottage cheese
3 tablespoons plain nonfat yogurt
½ cup chicken broth
2 tablespoons thinly sliced green onions
¼ teaspoon curry powder
1 cup coarsely chopped cauliflower florets
¼ cup thawed frozen peas
2 ounces cooked new potatoes, pared and coarsely chopped

In a large bowl, combine ¾ cup of flour, sugar, ¼ teaspoon of salt and paprika. With pastry blender or 2 knives, cut in margarine until mixture resembles coarse crumbs. Add cottage cheese and yogurt; stir until mixture forms soft ball. Gather dough into a ball; wrap in plastic wrap. Refrigerate several hours or overnight.

In large nonstick skillet, combine broth, green onions, the remaining ¼ teaspoon salt and the curry; cook over medium heat 2 minutes. Add cauliflower; cook, covered, 2 minutes. Stir in peas and potatoes; cook, covered 3 minutes, or until cauliflower is tender. Let cool to room temperature.

Preheat oven to 400 degrees. Spray cookie sheet with nonstick cooking spray.

Sprinkle clean work surface with the remaining 3 tablespoons of flour; roll dough into a 12-inch circle. With 4-inch biscuit cutter, cut out 4 circles. Reroll scraps of dough; continue cutting until all dough has been used, making a total of 8 circles.

Spoon about ¼ cup filling onto bottom half of each round, leaving a ¼-inch border. With a pastry brush, moisten bottom half of the border with water; fold top half of circle over filling to enclose. With fingers or tines of fork, press edges together to seal.

Arrange samosas on prepared baking sheet; bake 20 minutes or until crisp and golden brown. Serve immediately.

Yield: 4 servings

ACTIVITY – The Buffalo Zoo, Buffalo (Erie) – the "wildest place in town", is the nation's third oldest zoo. More than 1500 domestic and exotic animals live in this zoo, nestled in Olmsted's Delaware Park. It is open year round except for Thanksgiving and Christmas.

Oriental Beef Kabobs

28	(8-inch) wooden skewers
2	large garlic cloves
1	tablespoon finely grated peeled fresh gingerroot
¼	cup fresh lime juice, or to taste
8	ounces skirt steak
¼	cup hoisin sauce
1	tablespoon ketchup
	Lime wedges

Prepare grill. Soak skewers in warm water 20 minutes.

While skewers are soaking, thinly slice garlic and in a shallow glass dish stir together with gingerroot and 2 tablespoons lime juice. Season marinade with salt and pepper. Holding a knife at a 45 degree angle, cut steak crosswise into about ¼-inch thick slices and add to marinade, tossing to coat well. Marinate steak at room temperature 10 minutes.

In a small bowl whisk together hoisin sauce, ketchup, and remaining lime juice and season with salt and pepper. Drain skewers. Beginning at one end of each slice of steak, weave a skewer lengthwise through it, stretching slice on skewer to flatten, and transfer to a plate. Season sates with salt and pepper. Grill sates on an oiled rack set 5-6 inches over glowing coals 30 seconds to 1 minute on each side for medium-rare.

Serve steaks with hoisin dipping sauce and lime wedges.

FUN FACT – Limes are tart, but with a touch of sweetness; not as "puckery" as lemons. Select limes with firm smooth, shiny skin. Available year round.

Red Potato and Bacon Bites

1½ pounds small round red potatoes
4   slices of bacon
1   cup sour cream
½   teaspoon seasoned salt
¼   teaspoon pepper
1   tablespoon chopped fresh chives
½   cup shredded Cheddar cheese
     Parsley

Preheat the oven to 375 degrees. Place potatoes in saucepan and add enough water to cover. Bring to boil, and cook until tender but still firm, about 10 minutes. Drain, and cool in a bowl of cold water.

Cook bacon in a skillet over medium-high heat until evenly browned. Drain, crumble, and set aside.

Remove cooled potatoes from water. Pat dry with a paper towel and cut in half. Using a small spoon, carefully remove a small amount from center, leaving about ¼-inch rim around each potato. Set reserved potato aside.

In a bowl, mix together reserved potato, sour cream, bacon, seasoned salt, pepper and chives. Spoon a small amount of mixture into each potato half and place on a cookie sheet. Top each potato off with some shredded cheese.

Bake 10 minutes or until cheese is melted and potatoes are warmed through. Garnish with parsley and serve.

Yield: 40 servings

ACTIVITY – Frederick Olmsted was perhaps the greatest park designer in nineteenth century America. One of his masterpieces is <u>Delaware Park in Buffalo (Erie)</u>. It features 350 acres with a prominent water feature, a large meadow of 120 acres and significant wooded areas. Ideal for walking, jogging, picnicking, playing tennis and golf, or simply relaxing and enjoying nature.

Fresh Tomato Soup with Basil and Aïoli

2	garlic, peeled
2	cloves, peeled
⅓	cup fresh basil leaves, coarsely chopped
1	teaspoon lemon juice
¼	cup low calorie mayonnaise
1	tablespoon olive oil
1	cup onions, sliced
1	stalk celery, with leaves, thinly sliced diagonally
1	sprig basil
3	pounds tomatoes, peeled and halved
2	cups chicken stock
	Aïoli (olive oil)

With processor running, drop garlic through feed tube; chop finely. Add basil and lemon juice; chop finely. Add mayonnaise; blend.

Heat oil in heavy large saucepan over low heat. Add onion, celery, garlic and basil. Cover and cook until vegetables are very tender, stirring frequently, about 25 minutes.

Place large strainer over bowl and squeeze seeds and juice from tomatoes. Chop tomatoes and add to vegetables in saucepan. Using rubber spatula, press on tomato seeds and pulp in strainer to extract as much juice as possible. Add strained juice to saucepan. Add chicken stock to saucepan; bring to simmer over medium-low heat. Discard basil sprig. Ladle soup into bowls. Drizzle with aïoli.

FUN FACT – Since tomatoes are said to reduce the risk of heart attacks in half, extra sauce, light cheeses and vegetable toppings are a healthy alternative.

Tart Cherry Soup

2   cans (14½-ounces each) water-
     packed pitted tart cherries
½   cup orange juice
½   cup sugar
2   tablespoons lime juice
1   teaspoon grated lime peel
½   teaspoon ground cinnamon
4   lime slices

Place the cherries in a blender or food processor; cover and process until finely chopped. Transfer to a saucepan; add the orange juice, sugar, lime juice, peel and cinnamon. Bring to a boil. Reduce heat; cover and simmer for 10 minutes. Refrigerate until chilled. Garnish with lime slices.

Yield: 4 servings

ACTIVITY – <u>Six Flags Darien Lake, Darien Center (Genesee)</u> – is a huge amusement park about 20 miles from Buffalo. It has a performing arts center that seats 20,000.

Vichyssoise

2	cups finely diced raw potatoes
4	tablespoons butter
6	leeks, cleaned and cut into 1-inch pieces
3	cups chicken or vegetable stock
1	teaspoon salt
½	teaspoon freshly ground pepper
	Dash of nutmeg
1½-2	cups sour cream or heavy cream
	Chopped chives

Cook the potatoes in salted water to cover until just tender. Melt butter in a skillet and cool. Add leeks gently, tossing them lightly, for a few minutes. Add chicken bouillon and bring to boil. Lower heat and simmer the leeks until tender. Add potatoes to leeks and broth and season to taste with salt, pepper and nutmeg. Put mixture in blender (you will need to blend it in 2 lots) and blend for 1 minute or until smooth.

Chill. When ready to serve, mix in sour cream or heavy cream. Garnish with chopped chives.

Yield: 6 servings

FUN FACT – The white potato originated in the Andes Mountains and was probably brought to Britain by Sir Francis Drake about 1586.

Zucchini Soup

1	large onion, sliced
1	clove garlic, crushed
4	tablespoons butter
4	cups chopped zucchini
1	teaspoon dried basil
½	dried oregano
4	cups chicken stock
4	ounces cream cheese
	Salt and pepper to taste

In a large stock pot sauté onion and garlic in butter for 5 minutes. Add zucchini and herbs, cook over low heat for 5 minutes. Stir in chicken stock and heat through. Remove about 1 cup of the stock and combine with cream cheese in a blender or food processor until smooth. Return to pot, add salt and pepper to taste and simmer until heated through. Serve immediately.

ACTIVITY – The Balloons over Letchworth Co. gives hot air balloon rides over the scenic vistas of <u>Letchworth State Park, Castile (Wyoming)</u>. Seeing the majestic waterfalls from the air is especially impressive.

Easy Marshmallow Ambrosia

1   (8-ounce) container frozen whipped topping, thawed
1¼ cups shredded coconut
½   cup chopped walnuts
1   (8-ounce) can fruit cocktail, drained
1   (8-ounce) can pineapple chunks, drained
1   (11-ounce) can Mandarin oranges, drained
3   cups miniature marshmallows
1   (10-ounce) jar maraschino cherries, drained (optional)
½   teaspoon ground nutmeg
½   teaspoon ground cinnamon

In a large bowl, combine whipped topping, coconut, chopped nuts, fruit cocktail, pineapple, Mandarin oranges, marsh-mallows, cherries, nutmeg and cinnamon, mix well.

Refrigerate 30-45 minutes before serving.

Elegant Fresh Fruit Ambrosia

6   navel oranges
1   pineapple, peeled, cored and cut into cubes
1   cup coconut, shredded fresh, fresh frozen or packaged sweetened, according to taste/ availability
1   large banana
1   (4½-ounce) small bottle maraschino cherries, drained well (optional)

Peel the oranges, taking care to remove all the white pith. Slice the oranges over a bowl or storage container so that you catch any juice, and add the slices to the bowl. Circular slices look prettiest, hold together best, and are easiest.

Add the pineapple and coconut to the orange slices and gently toss.

Can be refrigerated up to 2 days, covered. When ready to serve, slice the banana and toss it with other fruits. Add the cherries last.

FITNESS FACT – Regular, moderate-to-brisk exercise can help reduce fatigue and manage stress.

Sensational Summer Salad

2	skinned cucumbers, diced
6	tomatoes cut into small wedges
1	large sweet red onion cut in thin strips
4	large sprigs of mint, finely chopped
2	bunches of parsley, finely chopped

Toss together and refrigerate.

Before serving, toss in a mixture of ¼ cup olive oil and ⅛ cup red wine.

ACTIVITY – <u>Panama Rocks, Panama (Chautauqua)</u> – The Panama Rock Scenic Park was formed when glaciers gouged the land 10,000 years ago. It has biking trails and picnic areas.

Basic Potato Salad

3 pounds Yukon gold or yellow potatoes, cooked, peeled and sliced or cubed for salad

3 tablespoons minced red onion

Mayonnaise to bind, regular or reduced fat

1 teaspoon sugar

1 teaspoon white vinegar

1 teaspoon dried dill or 1 tablespoon fresh chopped dill

Salt and pepper to taste

6 hard-boiled eggs, whites only, coarsely chopped

Combine potatoes, onion and blend in enough mayonnaise to make creamy and bind (1 cup or more). Add sugar, vinegar, dill, salt and pepper and blend well. Stir in chopped egg whites.

Chill.

FUN FACT – Summer Solstice is June 21st which is the longest day of the year in the northern hemisphere and the shortest day in the southern hemisphere, it marks the first day of summer.

Curried Chicken Salad

4	cups water
1¾	pounds skinless boneless chicken breast
½	cup mayonnaise
⅓	cup plain yogurt
5	teaspoons curry powder
1	tablespoon fresh lime juice
1	teaspoon honey
½	teaspoon ground ginger
½	teaspoon salt
¼	teaspoon black pepper
1	medium-sized red onion, chopped (1 cup)
1	firm-ripe mango or 2 small crisp apples (1 cup), peeled, pitted and chopped
1	cup red seedless grapes (5-ounce), halved
½	cup salted roasted cashews, coarsely chopped

Bring 4 cups of water to a simmer with chicken broth in a 2 to 3-quart saucepan. Add chicken and simmer, uncovered, 6 minutes. Remove pan from heat and cover, let stand until chicken is cooked through, about 15 minutes. Transfer chicken to a plate, cool 10 minutes, then chop into ½-inch pieces.

While chicken is cooling, in a large bowl whisk together mayonnaise, yogurt, curry, lime juice, honey, ginger, salt and pepper. Add chicken, onion, mango or apple, grapes, and cashews and stir gently to combine.

Serve chilled, best to refrigerate overnight to let the flavors meld.

ACTIVITY – Shakespeare in the Park is an annual July-August delight in Buffalo.

Basic Picnic Macaroni Salad

2	cups macaroni
2	eggs, hard-boiled and chopped
1	tablespoon green onion, minced
¼	cup sweet pickle, minced or 2 tablespoons relish
¼	cup celery, finely chopped
1	tablespoon capers
1	cup cooked green peas (use frozen, not canned)
2	tablespoons pimento, chopped

Dressing

½	cup mayonnaise
2	tablespoons pickle juice (do not use if relish is used)
1	teaspoon mustard, prepared
¼	teaspoon pepper
1	teaspoon salt
2	tablespoons sour cream
2	tablespoons parsley, chopped

Place macaroni in large bowl. Add egg, onion, pickle, celery, capers, peas, and pimentos.

Combine dressing ingredients and add to macaroni mixture. Toss lightly with 2 forks to combine.

Chill before serving.

FUN FACT – Americans spent an estimated $267 billion dining out in 1993.

Blueberry Corn Bread

1   cup flour, sifted
¾   cup cornmeal
2   tablespoons sugar
1   teaspoon baking powder
¾   teaspoon salt
1   cup blueberries, fresh or frozen
1   egg
⅔   cup milk, low fat
⅓   cup salad oil

Grease or spray 8 x 8-inch baking pan. Preheat oven to 425 degrees.

In bowl mix flour, cornmeal, sugar, baking powder, and salt. Stir in blueberries. In small bowl beat egg; add milk and oil, mix. Pour all at once into flour mixture. Stir just until dry ingredients are evenly moistened. Pour batter into baking pan. Bake 25 minutes or until golden.

ACTIVITY – <u>Toyfest USA, East Aurora (Erie)</u> – Celebrate the history of every child's favorite possession…Toys! Parades, car show and kids rides are all part of this 3 day festival.

Low-Fat Banana Bread

1½	cups all-purpose flour
1	cup whole wheat flour
2	teaspoons baking powder
1	teaspoon baking soda
1	teaspoon ground cinnamon
¼	teaspoon salt
6	ripe bananas, mashed
1	cup sugar
½	cup unsweetened applesauce
3	large egg whites
1	teaspoon vanilla extract
½	cup walnuts, finely chopped

Preheat oven to 350 degrees. Spray a 9 x 5-inch loaf pan with nonstick cooking spray.

In a medium bowl, whisk the flours, baking powder, baking soda, cinnamon and salt to combine. In another medium bowl, beat the mashed bananas, sugar, applesauce, egg whites, and vanilla until well mixed. Add the dry ingredients and whisk just until smooth. Stir in the walnuts. Transfer the batter to the loaf pan and smooth the top.

Bake for 50 minutes to 1 hour, until the top is browned and the sides of the bread pull away from the sides of the pan. Remove from the oven and let stand for 10 minutes on a wire baking rack. Invert and unmold onto the rack, turn right side up, and let cool completely.

FUN FACT – A banana that is yellow with no signs of green color is ready to be eaten raw. At this point, most all of the starch has been converted into sugar and the tasty banana can be easily digested.

Mango Bread

2 cups flour, sifted
2 teaspoons cinnamon
2 teaspoons baking soda
½ teaspoon salt
1¼ cups sugar
2 eggs
¾ cup oil
2½ cups chopped mango
 (about 3 large)
1 teaspoon lemon juice
½ cup raisins

Combine first 5 ingredients. In a small bowl beat eggs with oil and add to flour mixture. Stir in mangoes, lemon juice and raisins. Turn into 2 greased 8 x 4-inch loaf pans (or use one 12 cup Bundt pan) and bake at 350 degrees (325 degrees for glass pans) for one hour or until wooden pick inserted in center comes out clean.

ACTIVITY – <u>Fantasy Island, Grand Island (Erie)</u> – Grand Island in the Niagara River is home to Fantasy Island, an 80-acre theme park with around 100 rides and attractions.

Pineapple-Nut Bread

¾   cup packed brown sugar
3   tablespoons softened butter
2   eggs
2   cups flour
2   teaspoons baking powder
½   teaspoon salt
¼   teaspoon baking soda
8½ ounce can crushed pineapple
¾   cup chopped nuts
2   tablespoons sugar
½   teaspoon cinnamon

Cream brown sugar, butter and eggs until fluffy. Sift flour and blend with dry ingredients. Add ½ half the flour mixture into creamed mixture. Add pineapple and juice, and blend. Add the rest of the dry ingredients. Blend in nuts. Pour into a greased 9 x 5-inch loaf pan. Mix sugar and cinnamon for topping and sprinkle over the top of batter. Bake at 350 degrees for 45-50 minutes or until toothpick inserted in center comes out cleanly. Cool before slicing.

FUN FACT – The pineapple is a sign of hospitality.

Zucchini Nut Muffins

1½ cups all-purpose flour
¾ cup sugar
2 teaspoons baking powder
¼ teaspoon baking soda
¼ teaspoon salt
½ teaspoon ground cinnamon
2 large eggs
⅓ cup canola oil or almond oil
¼ cup orange marmalade
1 teaspoon vanilla extract (essence)
1 zucchini (4-ounce total weight) shredded and drained on paper towels
¾ cup dark raisins or dried sweet cherries
¼ cup pecans or almonds, chopped

Preheat oven to 400 degrees. Grease 10 standard muffin cups with butter or nonstick spray; fill unused cups ⅓ full with water to prevent warping.

In bowl stir together flour, sugar, baking powder, baking soda, salt, and cinnamon.

In another bowl whisk together eggs, oil, marmalade, vanilla, and zucchini until blended. Add dry ingredients to zucchini mixture in 3 increments and beat just until evenly moistened and smooth. Stir in raisins and nuts until evenly distributed. The batter will be stiff.

Spoon batter into each muffin cup, filling it no more than ¾ full.

Bake until golden brown, dry, springy to the touch, 17-20 minutes. A toothpick inserted into the center of a muffin should come out clean. Transfer the pan to a wire rack and let cool for 5 minutes. Unmold the muffins. Serve warm or room temperature with butter.

Yield: 10 muffins

ACTIVITY – Tifft Nature Preserve, Buffalo (Erie) – Take a nature walk on four different trails and enjoy the scenery of 264 acres including the undisturbed natural habitats of over 200 species of birds, wildlife, flowering annuals along with a 75 acre freshwater marsh.

Grilled Vegetable Skewers

1	medium ear fresh or frozen sweet corn, thawed and quartered
1	small zucchini, quartered
¼	small red onion, halved
4	cherry tomatoes
¼	teaspoon dried basil
¼	teaspoon dried rosemary, crushed
¼	teaspoon dried thyme
⅛	teaspoon garlic powder
⅛	teaspoon salt
⅛	teaspoon pepper

Place the corn on a microwave-safe plate. Cover with waxed paper. Microwave on high 2 minutes. If grilling the kabobs, coat grill rack with nonstick cooking spray before starting the grill. On 2 metal or soaked wooden skewers, alternately thread corn, zucchini, onion and tomatoes. Lightly coat vegetables with nonstick cooking spray. In a small bowl, combine seasonings; sprinkle over vegetables. Grill, covered, over medium heat or broil 4-6 inches from heat for 3 minutes on each side or until vegetables are tender, turning 3 times.

Yield: 2 servings

FITNESS FACT – Make cardiovascular fitness a lifetime commitment. Exercise, have good health and great fun.

Five-Veggie Stir-Fry

2	tablespoons cornstarch
2	tablespoons sugar
½	teaspoon ground ginger
1	cup orange juice
¼	cup reduced-sodium soy sauce
2	garlic cloves, minced
2	large carrots, sliced
2	cups broccoli florets
2	cups cauliflower florets
4	teaspoons olive or canola oil, divided
1	cup quartered fresh mushrooms
1	cup fresh or frozen snow peas
4	cups hot cooked rice

In a small bowl, combine the cornstarch, sugar and ginger. Stir in orange juice, soy sauce and garlic until blended; set aside. In a nonstick skillet or wok, stir-fry the carrots, broccoli and cauliflower in 3 teaspoons of oil for 4-5 minutes. Add mushrooms, peas and remaining oil; stir-fry for 3 minutes. Stir orange juice mixture and add to the pan. Bring to a boil; cook and stir until thickened. Serve over rice.

Yield: 4 servings

One serving (1 cup vegetable mixture with 1 cup rice) equals 382 calories, 5 grams fat (1 gram saturated fat), 0 cholesterol, 648 milligrams sodium, 74 grams carbohydrate, 3 grams fiber, 9 grams protein. Diabetic Exchange: 3 starch, 2 vegetable, 1 lean meat, 1 fat.

ACTIVITY – Strawberry Picking (Niagara, Genesee, Erie) – Pick your-own-farms are located all around Western New York. Strawberries most active picking season is June 1 to June 10. The end of the season would be around June 25.

Broccoli-Stuffed Tomatoes

1 ½	cups chopped fresh broccoli
4	medium tomatoes
1	teaspoon lemon juice
1	small onion, chopped
1	tablespoon butter or stick margarine
2	tablespoons all-purpose flour
½	cup 2% milk
¼	cup chicken broth
2	tablespoons grated Parmesan cheese
1	tablespoon minced fresh basil or ½ teaspoon dried basil
¼	teaspoon salt
⅛	teaspoon pepper
1	egg white

In a saucepan, bring broccoli and 1-inch of water to a boil. Reduce heat; cover and simmer for 3-4 minutes or until crisp-tender. Drain and set aside. Cut a ½-inch slice off the top of each tomato; with a spoon or melon baler, hollow out each tomato leaving a ½-inch shell. Discard pulp. Sprinkle ¼ teaspoon lemon juice into each tomato; place upside down on paper towel 10 minutes to drain.

In a skillet, sauté onion in butter until tender. In a bowl, combine flour, milk and broth until smooth. Stir into onion mixture. Bring to boil; cook and stir 2 minutes or until thickened. Remove from heat; stir in Parmesan cheese, basil, salt, pepper and reserved broccoli. In a mixing bowl, beat egg white until stiff peaks form. Fold into broccoli mixture.

Place tomatoes in an ungreased 8-inch square baking dish. Spoon the broccoli mixture into each tomato, mounding in the center. Bake, uncovered at 350 degrees for 30-35 minutes or until a knife inserted near the center comes out clean and the tops are golden brown.

Yield: 4 servings

FUN FACTS – Broccoli sprouts contain from 10-100 times more cancer-fighting compounds than mature broccoli. One-fourth cup of sprouts gives you the benefits of six and one-half cups of chopped broccoli. The taste is much different for those who don't like broccoli and they go well in salads and on sandwiches.

Basil Fettuccine

8	ounces uncooked fettuccine
1	(8-ounce) cup fat-free plain yogurt
¼	cup grated Parmesan cheese
2	tablespoons chopped fresh basil
	or 2 teaspoons dried basil
½	teaspoon salt
¼	teaspoon pepper
2	garlic cloves, minced
1	tablespoon olive or canola oil

Cook fettuccine according to package directions. In a bowl, combine yogurt, Parmesan cheese, basil, salt and pepper; set aside. In a small nonstick skillet, sauté garlic in oil 1 minute. Drain fettuccine and place in a large bowl. Add garlic and oil; toss. Add yogurt mixture; toss until well coated. Serve immediately.

Yield: 4 servings

ACTIVITY – Township Summer Concert Series – Enjoy free concerts during the summer in towns throughout Western New York.

Basil Caesar Salmon

4	salmon fillets (8-ounces each)
¼	cup creamy Caesar salad dressing
	Pepper to taste
1	cup Caesar salad croutons, crushed
½	cup grated Parmesan cheese
2	teaspoons dried basil
2	tablespoons olive oil

Place salmon in a greased 15 x 10-inch baking pan. Spoon the salad dressing over fillets; sprinkle with pepper. Combine the croutons, Parmesan cheese and basil; sprinkle over fillets and gently press into dressing. Drizzle with oil. Bake, uncovered, at 350 degrees for 15-20 minutes or until fish flakes easily with a fork.

Yield: 4 servings

FUN FACT – There are over 240 varieties of fish and shellfish sold in the fish markets and grocery stores!

Glass Noodles with Chicken and Shrimp

Dressing

½	cup sugar
¼	cup Thai fish sauce
3	tablespoons light brown sugar
2	tablespoons cider vinegar
½	cup lime juice
1	tablespoon minced cilantro stems
2	teaspoons minced serrano chile
1	garlic clove, minced

Noodles

2	ounces uncooked bean threads (cellophane noodles)
2	cup cooked, peeled, chopped shrimp (about ½ pound)
6	ounce cooked chicken breast, cut into ¼-inch strips
2	cup torn romaine lettuce
1	cup chopped tomato
½	cup sliced onion
⅓	cup sliced celery
2	tablespoons chopped, dry roasted peanuts
4	teaspoons minced serrano chile

For dressing: combine first 4 ingredients in a saucepan. Bring to boil and cook for 2 minutes or until sugar dissolves. Cool, stir in lime juice, 1 tablespoon cilantro, 1 teaspoon chile and garlic.

For noodles: cook noodles in boiling water 1½ minutes, drain. Rinse under cold water. Drain. Coarsely chop noodles. Combine noodles, shrimp and next 5 ingredients (shrimp through celery) in a large bowl. Drizzle dressing over noodles, toss gently to coat. Sprinkle with peanuts, 2 tablespoons cilantro and 2 teaspoons chile.

Yield: 5 servings (serving size 1 cup)

ACTIVITY – Thursday at the Square, Buffalo (Erie) – Enjoy a series of free concerts throughout the summer. Acts include local talent as well as National headliners.

South-of-the-Boarder Pizza

1	tablespoon cornmeal
1	(1-pound) loaf frozen bread dough, thawed
½	pound lean ground beef
1	medium onion, chopped
1	yellow pepper, chopped
1	garlic clove, minced
1	(16-ounce) can fat-free refried beans
1	cup salsa
1	(4-ounce) can chopped green chilies
1-2	teaspoons chili powder
2	(8-ounce) cups shredded reduced-fat Mexican-blend cheese
2	medium tomatoes, chopped
2	cups shredded lettuce

Coat 2 (12-inch) pizza pans with nonstick cooking spray; sprinkle with cornmeal. Divide the bread dough in half; roll each portion into a 12-inch circle. Transfer to prepared pans. Build up edges slightly; prick dough thoroughly with a fork. Bake at 425 degrees for 12 minutes or until lightly browned.

Meanwhile, in a skillet, cook beef, onion, yellow pepper and garlic over medium heat until meat is no longer pink; drain. Stir in refried beans, salsa, chilies and chili powder; heat through. Spread over crusts; sprinkle with cheese. Bake 6-7 minutes longer or until cheese is melted. Top with tomatoes and lettuce; serve immediately.

Yield: 2 pizzas (6 slices each)

One slice equals 250 calories, 7 grams fat (3 grams saturated fat), 20 milligrams cholesterol, 706 milligrams sodium, 31 grams carbohydrate, 5 gram fiber, 17 grams protein. Diabetic Exchanges: 2 lean meat, 1½ starch, 1 vegetable.

FUN FACT – The 10 most popular pizza toppings by country are: Squid (Japan), tuna and corn (England), black bean sauce (Guatemala), mussels and clams (Chile), barbecued chicken (Bahamas), eggs (Australia), pickled ginger (India), fresh cream (France), green peas (Brazil), and guava (Colombia).

Orange Pork with Leeks and Trio of Peppers

4 (4-ounces each, ½-inch thick) boneless center-cut pork chop loins
½ teaspoon sugar
¼ teaspoon salt
¼ teaspoon fresh ground black pepper
2 teaspoons vegetable oil
3½ cups leeks (about 4 medium-sized leeks), thinly sliced cross-wise (so you have small round discs)
1½ cups mixed green, red and yellow bell peppers, cut into ¼-inch strips
3 garlic cloves, minced
¾ cup fat-free, low sodium chicken broth
3 tablespoons orange juice concentrate, thawed
1 tablespoon Dijon mustard
¼ teaspoon crushed red pepper

Sprinkle pork chop loins evenly with sugar, salt and black pepper. In a large non-stick skillet, heat oil over medium heat. Add pork and sauté each side until cooked through (about 2½ minutes each side). Remove pork, set aside and keep warm.

In same skillet add leeks, peppers and garlic, sauté until leeks are tender, about 2-4 minutes. Stir in broth, juice concentrate, mustard and red pepper, cook until liquid thickens, scraping skillet to loosen browned bits, about 2½ minutes. Return pork to skillet, turning to coat both sides. Serve immediately

One pork chop loin and ⅓ cup leek and pepper mixture

Calories 266, fat 10 grams (saturated 3 grams), protein 24 grams, carbohydrates 20 grams, fiber 2 grams

ACTIVITY – Try a bicycle or canoe for an Erie Canal trek, starting at Medina (Orleans).

Broccoli with Roasted Red Peppers

5	cups broccoli florets (about 1 large bunch)
1-2	garlic cloves, minced
1	tablespoon butter or stick margarine
¼	cup diced roasted red peppers
1	tablespoon minced fresh parsley
½	teaspoon salt
⅛	teaspoon pepper

Place broccoli in a steamer basket. Place in a saucepan over 1-inch of water; bring to boil. Cover and steam 5-8 minutes or until crisp-tender. In nonstick skillet sauté garlic in butter. Stir in red peppers, parsley, salt and pepper. Transfer broccoli to a large bowl; add red pepper mixture and toss to coat.

Yield: 6 servings

Steamed Baby Carrots

1½	cups baby carrots
2	teaspoons brown sugar
1	teaspoon butter or stick margarine
1	teaspoon white wine vinegar or cider vinegar
⅛	teaspoon salt
1	teaspoon minced chives

Place carrots in a steamer basket. Place in a saucepan over 1-inch of water; bring to boil. Cover and steam 5-8 minutes or until tender. Transfer carrots to a bowl. Add brown sugar, butter, vinegar and salt; toss until butter is melted and carrots are coated. Sprinkle with chives.

Yield: 2 servings

FITNESS FACT – The average calories spent jumping rope by a 150-pound person are 750 calories per hour. A lighter person burns fewer calories; a heavier person burns more.

Vegetable Couscous

2	medium carrots, diced
½	cup diced celery
1	medium onion, diced
¼	cup julienned yellow pepper
¼	cup julienned sweet red pepper
2	tablespoons olive or canola oil
1	medium zucchini, diced
¼	cup minced fresh basil or 4 teaspoons dried basil
¼	teaspoon garlic salt
⅛	teaspoon pepper
	Dash hot pepper sauce
1	cup uncooked couscous
1½	cups chicken broth

In a large skillet, sauté carrots, celery, onion and peppers in oil 5-6 minutes or until crisptender. Add next 5 ingredients; mix well. Stir in couscous. Add broth; bring to boil. Cover and remove from heat; let stand 5-8 minutes. Fluff with fork and serve immediately.

Yield: 4 servings

Garlic Smashed Red Potatoes

2½	pounds red potatoes (about 8 medium), quartered
3	garlic cloves, peeled
2	tablespoons butter or stick margarine
½	cup fat-free milk, warmed
½	teaspoon salt
¼	cup grated Parmesan cheese

Place potatoes and garlic in a large saucepan; cover with water. Bring to boil. Reduce heat; cover and simmer 20-25 minutes or until potatoes are very tender. Drain well. Add butter, milk and salt; mash. Stir in Parmesan cheese.

Yield: 6 servings

ACTIVITY – Buffalo Garden Walk, Buffalo (Erie) – Buffalo residents open their beautiful home gardens for others to enjoy. Garden walk encourages neighborhood beautification, helps improve urban environment and affirms a sense of community.

Carrot and Celery Amandine

1	garlic clove, minced
1	teaspoon canola oil
1	tablespoon water
1	tablespoon reduced-sodium soy sauce
½	teaspoon sugar
1¼	cups sliced carrots
½	cup chopped onion
⅓	cup chopped celery
2	tablespoons sliced almonds, toasted

In a large nonstick skillet, sauté garlic in oil 1 minute or until tender. Stir in water, soy sauce and sugar. Bring to boil. Add carrots, onion and celery; cook until crisp-tender. Sprinkle with almonds.

Yield: 2 servings

Gingered Squash Sauté

1	pound yellow summer squash
½	pound small zucchini, sliced
1	medium onion, thinly sliced
1	medium green pepper, julienned
4	teaspoons butter or stick margarine
3	medium tomatoes, peeled and quartered
¾	teaspoon salt
½-1	teaspoon ground ginger

Cut yellow squash in half lengthwise, then into ½-inch slices. In a large skillet, sauté squash, zucchini, onion, and green pepper in butter 1 minute. Cover and cook over medium heat 3 minutes. Add tomatoes, salt and ginger. Cover and cook 2-3 minutes or until heated through.

Yield: 9 servings

FITNESS FACT – Circuit training, in which you move quickly from one strengthening maneuver to the next, burns calories faster than walking does. And your body continues to burn calories for hours after any type of strength training. More important, the muscle you build consumes calories more rapidly, even when you're not exercising.

Roasted Brussels Sprouts

2	pounds fresh or frozen Brussels sprouts, thawed
1	tablespoon butter or stick margarine
1	tablespoon olive or canola oil
½	teaspoon salt
¼	teaspoon pepper

Cut an "X" in the core end of each Brussels sprout with a sharp knife. Place 1-inch of water in a saucepan; add sprouts. Bring to boil. Reduce heat; cover and simmer 5-6 minutes or until crisp-tender. Drain. Add remaining ingredients and toss to coat.

Arrange sprouts in a single layer in a 15 x 10 x 1-inch baking pan coated with nonstick cooking spray. Bake, uncovered, at 425 degrees for 15-20 minutes, stirring occasionally. Serve immediately.

Yield: 6 servings

Corn Fritter Patties

1	cup pancake mix
1	egg, beaten
¼	cup plus 2 tablespoons milk
1	(7-ounce) can whole kernel corn, drained
2	cups vegetable oil

In a small bowl, combine pancake mix, egg and milk just until moistened. Stir in corn. In an electric skillet, heat ¼-inch oil over medium heat. Drop batter by ¼ cupfuls into oil; press lightly to flatten. Cook 2 minutes on each side or until golden brown.

Yield: 7 patties

ACTIVITY – Porter Cup, Lewiston (Niagara) – The Porter Cup, held at Niagara Falls Country Club, ranks as one of the top Invitational Amateur golf tournaments in the world.

43

Simple Peach Cobbler

6   peaches, peeled and sliced thinly
1   cup sugar
1   cup milk
2   sticks butter, melted
1   cup flour
    Nutmeg and cinnamon

Preheat oven to 400 degrees. Place peaches in a greased 9 x 12-inch pan. Pour remaining ingredients on top of peaches. Bake for 35-40 minutes or until top is browned and crispy.

FUN FACT – Sometimes Frozen Fruits and Vegetables are More Nutritious than Fresh! The longer that fruits or vegetables sit around waiting to be sold or eaten, the more nutrients they lose. But fruits and vegetables grown for freezing are usually frozen right after they are picked. Therefore, they have less time to lose their nutrients.

Simple Fruit Trifle

2   cups angel food cake cut into 1-inch cubes

½   cup strong, cooled coffee

1   cup vanilla yogurt

2   cups fresh seasonal berries (Ex. blueberries, strawberries, raspberries)

½   cup sliced plum or peach

¼   cup granola

2   tablespoons wheat germ (optional)

Arrange angel food cake cubes on a baking sheet and drizzle with the coffee, turning to moisten all sides.

In a 2-quart serving bowl or 4 (8-ounce) glasses or bowls, layer angel food cake, yogurt, berries, plum or peach slices.

Sprinkle granola and wheat germ on top. Chill for 10 minutes before serving.

Yield: 4 servings

One cup serving contains 330 calories, 7 grams carbohydrates, 3 grams fiber, 9 grams protein, 1 gram fat

ACTIVITY – <u>Pick your own Blueberries</u> at select farms in Chautauqua, Niagara, and Erie counties. The most active picking season for blueberries is July 5th through August 10th.

45

Roasted Peach Pies with Cream

Pastry Rounds

1	cup all-purpose flour
1½	teaspoons sugar
	Pinch of kosher salt
1	stick cold unsalted butter, cut into small pieces
2	tablespoons ice water

Filling

4	large peaches (about 6-ounces each), sliced ½-inch thick
½	cup granulated sugar
1	cup heavy cream
1	tablespoon confectioners' sugar, plus more for sprinkling

Make the pastry rounds: In a food processor, pulse the flour with the sugar and salt. Add the butter and pulse until the mixture resembles coarse meal. Drizzle the water over the mixture and pulse just until a dough forms. Turn the dough out onto a lightly floured surface and pat it into a disk. Wrap in plastic and refrigerate for at least 30 minutes.

Preheat the oven to 425 degrees. Cut the dough into 8 equal pieces. Working with 1 piece at a time and keeping the rest refrigerated, roll the dough between 2 sheets of wax paper into a 4-inch round. Refrigerate the pastry round and repeat with the remaining dough.

Arrange the pastry rounds on a baking sheet and bake about 15 minutes, or until golden brown. Transfer to a rack and let cool.

Make the filling: Butter a large rimmed baking sheet. Spread the peaches on the sheet and sprinkle with the granulated sugar. Roast for 15 minutes, or until the peaches are soft and slightly browned at the edges; let cool.

In a medium bowl, beat the heavy cream with the 1 tablespoon of confectioners' sugar until soft peaks form. Place 4 of the pastry rounds on plates. Top them with half of the peaches and half of the whipped cream. Lay a second pastry round on the cream and top with the remaining peaches and whipped cream. Sprinkle with confectioners' sugar and serve immediately.

FUN FACT – The top 10 beverages requested in restaurants are: Cappuccino, mineral water, lemonade, Expresso, flavored coffee, fruit juice blends, beer, flavored water, iced tea, and hot coffee.

Raspberry Pie with Oat Crust

Crust

¾	cup all-purpose flour
½	cup quick cooking oats
½	teaspoon salt
¼	canola oil
3-4	tablespoons cold water

Filling

2	cups water
1	(8-ounce) package sugar-free cook and serve vanilla pudding mix
1	(3-ounce) package sugar-free raspberry gelatin
4	cups fresh raspberries

For crust: Preheat oven to 400 degrees.

In a food processor combine flour, oats and salt. While processing, slowly drizzle in oil. Gradually add oil until ball forms. Roll out dough between two sheets of waxed paper. Remove top sheet of waxed paper and flip remaining waxed paper and dough onto 9-inch pie tin. Remove remaining waxed paper and trim, seal and flute crust edges.

Bake at 400 degrees until golden brown, about 10-12 minutes.

Cool completely on a wire rack.

For filling: In a medium saucepan, heat water over medium heat and whisk in pudding mix.

Cook and stir until thickened and bubbly, about 5 minutes. Whisk in gelatin until completely dissolved and remove from heat. Cool slightly, fold in raspberries and spoon into crust. Chill for at least 8 hours

Yield: 8 servings

167 calories, 8 grams fat (1 gram saturated fat), 22 grams carbohydrates, 5 grams fiber, 3 grams protein

ACTIVITY – Allentown Art Show, Buffalo (Erie) – Hundreds of juried artists and crafters display and sell their art to the hundreds of thousands of visitors during this summer weekend event. This outdoor festival takes place in the Allentown Historic Preservation District of Buffalo.

Chocolate Cake

4	ounces unsweetened chocolate
½	cup milk
¼	teaspoon Jamaican allspice
1	cup brown sugar, packed
1	egg yolk
1	teaspoon baking soda
½	teaspoon salt
2	cups cake flour
8	tablespoons butter
1	cup superfine sugar
2	egg yolks
3	tablespoon water
½	cup milk
1	teaspoon vanilla
1	tablespoon dark rum
2	egg whites, whipped

Preheat oven to 350 degrees. Grease 2 (9-inch) layer cake pans.

Whisk together chocolate, milk, brown sugar, allspice and 1 egg yolk in the top of a double boiler, stirring until a custard is formed and mixture thickens. Cool. Stir in baking soda and salt. Sift the flour onto waxed paper.

In bowl of electric mixer, whip the butter, gradually adding sugar and 2 egg yolks, one at a time, beating well after each addition. In a cup, stir together 3 tablespoons water, ½ cup milk, and 1 teaspoon vanilla extract and 1 tablespoon dark rum.

Add the flour mixture to the butter mixture alternating with the vanilla/milk/water mixture. Stir in the chocolate custard mixture and beat until smooth, approximately 2-3 minutes at medium speed of mixer.

In a clean bowl, using the wire whisk attachment of your electric mixer beat 2 egg whites until soft peaks form; gently fold into cake batter. Turn into greased layer cake pans. Bake at 350 degrees for about 25 minutes or until cake tester or toothpick inserted in center comes out clean.

Turn out onto wire racks to cool. Level with a serrated knife if required, then stack and frost with chocolate frosting.

FUN FACT – Chocolate can be lethal to dogs. About two ounces of milk chocolate can be poisonous for a ten pound puppy because it affects the cardiac muscle and central nervous system.

Carrot Pineapple Cake

4	eggs
2	cups sugar
1½	cups oil
2	cups sifted self-rising flour
2	teaspoons cinnamon
2	cups finely grated carrots
1	(8¼-ounce) crushed pineapple, undrained
¾	cup chopped pecans

Cream cheese frosting for cake

1	(8-ounce) package cream cheese
8	tablespoons softened butter
4	cups powdered sugar
2	teaspoons vanilla

Preheat oven to 325 degrees. Grease and flour a 13 x 9 x 2-inch pan.

Beat eggs in large mixing bowl. Add sugar and oil, beat until well blended. Stir in flour and cinnamon. Blend well. Stir in carrots and undrained pineapple and pecans. Pour in pan and bake 55-60 minutes or until cake pulls away from pan. Cool and frost.

For frosting: Beat cream cheese and butter together. Gradually add sugar and beat until smooth. Add vanilla. Mix well. Spread over cake.

ACTIVITY – The Lucy-Desi Museum is in Lucy's hometown, Jamestown (Chautauqua). Lucy-Desi Days Memorial Day Weekend and Lucy's birthday celebration in early August are events that are a ball!

Blueberry Pound Cake

2	sticks butter, softened (note do not substitute margarine)
2	cups sugar
4	eggs, room temperature
1	teaspoon vanilla extract
1	teaspoon baking powder
1	teaspoon salt
2	cups blueberries
	Flour for coating

Preheat oven to 325 degrees. Grease two 5 x 9-inch loaf pans and coat with sugar.

Using and electric mixer, cream the butter and sugar until light and fluffy. Add eggs one at a time and beat well before adding next egg. Add vanilla and mix well.

Beat in flour one cup at a time, batter will become thick. Add baking soda and salt, mix well.

Coat blueberries in flour and gently stir into batter with a wooden spoon. Divide batter in half and spread equal amounts into each loaf pan. Bake for 1 hour, cool on wire rack for at least 30 minutes before removing from pan.

FUN FACT – White chocolate is not really chocolate at all. It is made from vanilla, sugar and cream, not cocoa beans. Natural and artificial flavors are added for a chocolate taste.

Chocolate Marble Meringues

3   ounces bittersweet chocolate
4   egg whites
1   cup sugar

Preheat oven to 275 degrees. Line 2 baking sheets with parchment paper.

In saucepan bring 1-2 inches of water to a simmer. Place chocolate in a heatproof bowl over, but not touching, simmering water and stir occasionally until melted.

Set aside and cool slightly.

Combine egg whites and sugar in another heatproof bowl over, but not touching, simmering water and whisk until mixture is hot, about 4-5 minutes. Remove bowl from heat and using electric mixer beat on high until stiff peaks from and mixture is lukewarm, about 4-5 minutes.

Drizzle melted chocolate over egg white mixture and fold in with a rubber spatula until mixture is just marbled.

Using a soup spoon drop batter in 20 large mounds about 1½ to 2-inches apart on parchment paper covered baking sheets. Bake at 275 degrees until crispy outside and chewy inside, about 35-40 minutes. Transfer baking sheet to wire racks to cool, do not remove meringues from parchment paper until completely cooled.

Store in an airtight container.

ACTIVITY – Allegany County Fair, Angelica (Allegany) – rides, livestock competition, demonstrations, tractor pulls, contests, entertainment, demolition derby, food and fun.

Thick and Chewy Chocolate Chip Cookies

2⅛ cups (2 cups plus 2 tablespoons) unsifted bleached all-purpose flour

½ teaspoon salt

½ teaspoon baking soda

1½ sticks unsalted butter, melted and cooled until warm

1 cup brown sugar (light or dark)

½ cup granulated sugar

1 large egg plus 1 egg yolk

2 teaspoons vanilla extract

1-2 cups semi- or bittersweet chocolate chips/chunks

1 cup raisins, nuts or coconut (optional, a combination is great too, just make sure it is not more than 1 cup)

Line two 20 x 14-inch lipless cookie sheets with parchment paper. Adjust oven racks to upper- and lower-middle positions and preheat oven to 325 degrees. Line 2 lipless cookie sheets.

In a medium bowl mix flour, salt, and baking soda and set aside.

In a large bowl, by hand or with electric mixer, mix butter and sugars until thoroughly blended.

Add egg, yolk, and vanilla and mix. Add dry ingredients; mix until just combined. Stir in chips and optional raisins, nuts or coconut to taste.

Form ¼ cups of dough into balls. Hold dough ball using fingertips of both hands and pull into 2 equal halves. Re-join the halves by gently pressing the smooth sides together, leaving pulled sides "rough". Place on parchment paper-lined lipless cookie sheets, about 9 dough balls per sheet.

Dough can be refrigerated up to 2 days or frozen up to 1 month-shaped or not.

Bake at 325 degrees, reversing cookie sheets' positions halfway through baking (about 7-9 minutes), until cookies are light golden brown and outer edges start to harden yet centers are still soft and puffy, about 15-18 minutes total (start checking at 13 minutes).

Cool cookies on cookie sheets placed on a wire rack. Serve or store in airtight container.

Yield: 1½ dozen 3-inch cookies

Special Equipment: Parchment paper

FUN FACT – The International Ice Cream Association reports that in the average household, 66% of the ice cream is eaten by adults.

Apple Cranberry Crisp

Topping

1	cup (packed) golden brown sugar
1	cup old-fashioned oats
¾	cup all-purpose flour
¼	teaspoon salt
1	stick chilled unsalted butter, cut into pieces

Filling

1	(12-ounce) package cranberries
1¾	pounds Golden Delicious or Fuji apples (about 4 medium-sized), peeled, cored, cut into ½-inch cubes
1½	cups sugar
2	tablespoons apple juice or cider
	Vanilla ice cream

For topping: Combine brown sugar, oats, flour, and salt in large bowl; toss to blend. Add butter and rub in with fingertips until mixture comes together in moist clumps. Cover; chill while preparing filling. (Topping can be prepared 1 day ahead; keep chilled.)

For filling: Preheat oven to 375 degrees. Generously butter 13 x 9 x 2-inch glass baking dish. Combine cranberries, apples, sugar, and apple juice in heavy large pot. Bring to boil over medium heat, stirring often. Boil until cranberries are tender and juices thicken slightly, about 5 minutes. Transfer filling to prepared dish. Sprinkle topping over.

Bake crisp until filling bubbles thickly and topping is crisp and deep golden brown, about 40 minutes. Let cool 10 minutes. Serve with ice cream.

Yield: 12 servings

ACTIVITY – Midway Amusement Park, Maple Springs (Chautauqua) – has been a family mecca for more than a century. Go-carts, bumper boats and other rides as well as the historical memorabilia are pleasing to both children and adults.

Strawberries Romanoff

2   pints strawberries, washed and stemmed
¼   cup sugar
¼   cup orange liqueur, such as Grand Marnier or Cointreau
1   pint vanilla ice cream
1   cup heavy cream

Slice the strawberries. In a large bowl, toss ¾ of them with the sugar and orange liqueur. Refrigerate at least 1 hour to macerate.

Put the ice cream in the refrigerator to soften.

Put the cream and half the macerated strawberries in a cold mixing bowl. With an electric mixer, whip to soft peaks, about 12 minutes. Fold in the ice cream.

Distribute the cream among 6 chilled bowls. Mix the plain sliced berries with the remaining macerated berries and place on top of the cream.

Yield: 6-8 servings

FUN FACT – Red, ripe, juicy strawberries don't just taste great, they're good for you, too! Eight medium berries provide 160% of the daily value for vitamin C (more than one orange), and they're an excellent source of fiber.

Lite Strawberry Mousse

4   cups fresh or frozen strawberries,
        quartered
½   cup sugar
1   (1-ounce) package sugar free
        instant vanilla pudding mix
1   (8-ounce) cup fat-free whipped
        topping

In a food processor or blender combine strawberries and sugar until smooth. Add pudding mix and process until smooth. Transfer to a large mixing bowl if necessary and fold in whipped topping.

Spoon equal amounts (½ cup) into dessert dishes.

145 calories, 3 grams fat (3 grams saturated), 27 grams carbohydrates, 2 grams fiber.

ACTIVITY – <u>Polish American Festival</u> – Celebrate the Polish-American heritage at this festival. Enjoy traditional food, crafts, workshops and entertainment.

Cool Watermelon Slush

8	cups cubed seedless watermelon
¼	cup lime juice
¼	cup sugar
2	cups diet lemon-lime soda, chilled

In a blender or food processor combine watermelon, lime juice and sugar until smooth.

Pour into a freezer proof container until edges begin to freeze, about 30 minutes. Stir and return to freezer, repeat every 20 minutes until slushy, about 90 minutes. Pour or scoop ¾ of a cup into bowls or glasses and add ¼ of a cup of soda.

75 calories, 1 gram fat, 18 grams carbohydrates, 1 gram fiber, 4 gram protein

Watermelon Ice

⅓	cup water
½	cup sugar
3	pound piece chilled watermelon
1	tablespoon fresh lemon juice

In a small saucepan simmer water with sugar, stirring until sugar is dissolved. Transfer syrup to a bowl set in a larger bowl of ice and cold water and stir syrup until cold.

Discard rind from watermelon and cut fruit into 1-inch chunks. In a blender purée watermelon, syrup, and lemon juice and pour through a fine sieve into a 9-inch square metal baking pan, pressing hard on solids. Freeze mixture, covered, until frozen, 6-8 hours, and up to 2 days. Just before serving, scrape watermelon ice with a fork to lighten texture and break up ice crystals.

Yield: 6 servings

FUN FACT – You can count on finding watermelon, honeydew and cantaloupes almost year-round, though specialty melons have a season that peaks from mid-July to mid-September.

Ice Cream "Less" Banana Split

2   cups reduced fat graham cracker crumbs (about 32 squares)

5   tablespoons reduced fat margarine

1   (12-ounce) can cold reduced fat evaporated milk

¼   cup cold fat-free milk

2   packages (1-ounce each) sugar-free instant vanilla pudding mix

2   medium-sized firm bananas cut in to ½-inch slices

1   (20-ounce) can unsweetened crushed pineapple, drained

1   (8-ounce) cup fat-free whipped topping

3   tablespoons chopped walnuts

3   tablespoons chocolate syrup

5   maraschino cherries, quartered

Coat 13 x 9 x 2-inch baking dish with non-stick cooking spray.

Combine graham cracker crumbs and margarine and press into bottom of baking dish. In a large bowl, whisk together evaporated milk, fat-free milk and pudding mix until slightly thickened, about 2 minutes. Spread mixture evenly over crust.

Layer bananas, pineapple and whipped topping. Sprinkle with nuts, drizzle with chocolate syrup and top with maraschino cherries.

Refrigerate for at least 1 hour before serving.

Yield: 15 servings

194 calories, 6 grams fat (3 grams saturated fat), 33 grams carbohydrates, 1 gram fiber, 3 gram protein.

ACTIVITY – Artpark, Lewiston (Niagara) – Located in a state park above the Niagara gorge, Artpark offers Broadway musicals, band concerts, celebrity performances, free concerts in the amphitheater, and festivals. Hiking trails, fishing docks and picnic areas may also be enjoyed.

Yogurt-Sicles

2	(16-ounce) cups strawberry reduced fat yogurt
1	(8-ounce) can unsweetened crushed pineapple
1	tablespoon honey

In a blender or food processor combine all ingredients and process until smooth.

Pour ¼ cup into each of 10 plastic molds or 10 paper cups. Insert holders or Popsicle sticks.

Freeze until firm, about 8 hours.

61 calories, 13 grams carbohydrates, 2 grams protein

Fuzzy Navel Smoothie

1½	cups frozen sliced peaches
½	cup frozen orange juice concentrate
½	cup 1% milk
⅓	cup sliced banana
1	teaspoon sugar
	Dash (less than ⅛ teaspoon) of salt
	Orange slices (optional)

Pour peaches, orange juice concentrate, milk, banana, sugar and salt into blender, let stand for 15 minutes then process until smooth. Pour into glasses and serve immediately, garnishing with orange slices if desired.

Yield: 2 (1 cup) servings

Calories 223, fat 1 gram, protein 5 grams, carbohydrates 50 grams, fiber 3 grams

ACTIVITY – <u>Gerry Rodeo (Chautauqua)</u> – This is the oldest running rodeo east of the Mississippi.

Spring

Spring

Feta Pastry Puffs

1   (17¼-ounce) package sheet puff pastry, thawed

       All-purpose flour for dusting

3½   ounces feta, crumbled (scant ½ cup)

1   tablespoon heavy cream or ½ tablespoon whole milk

⅛   teaspoon pepper

1   large egg, slightly beaten

1½   tablespoons fresh thyme leaves

Preheat oven to 425 degrees.

Roll out pastry into a 14 x 10-inch rectangle (about ⅛-inch thick) on a lightly floured surface. Trim edges, preferably with a pizza wheel, and cut pastry lengthwise into 6 (1½-inch-wide) strips. Chill strips on a cookie sheet, covered with plastic wrap, until cold, about 10 minutes.

Blend feta, cream, pepper, and 1 tablespoon egg in a food processor until smooth, then form into 21 balls on a work surface.

Keeping remaining pastry covered, brush top of 1 strip with some of beaten egg. Starting ½-inch from one end and leaving ½-inch at opposite end, evenly space 7 cheese balls down center of strip. Cover with another pastry strip, pressing ends together, then press between balls of filling gently but firmly. Press pastry around each ball to seal top and bottom together and wipe away any filling that leaks out. Brush top of strip (but not sides) with some of egg and sprinkle with ½ tablespoon thyme. Cut between mounds of filling to form squares and arrange pastries 1-inch apart on a parchment-lined cookie sheet. Make more pastries with remaining strips, filling, and thyme.

Bake about 12 minutes in middle of oven or until puffed and golden. Serve warm.

Unbaked pastries can be frozen, wrapped well in plastic wrap for up to two weeks and must be thawed in the refrigerator when ready for use.

ACTIVITY – <u>Akron Falls State Park, Akron (Erie)</u> – has hiking trails and picnic facilities in addition to its famous waterfall.

7-Layer Dip

1	(16-ounce) container sour cream
1	(1.25-ounce) package taco seasoning
1½	(16-ounce) cans refried beans
1	cup salsa
2	cups lettuce, shredded
1	large tomato, chopped
2	avocados, diced
½	cup green onions, chopped
2	cups shredded cheese
1	(4-ounce) can sliced black olives

Mix sour cream and taco seasoning. Chill in fridge for 30 minutes.

In sauce pan, combine Refried Beans and salsa. Heat on medium until evenly blended. Let cool.

Shred lettuce. Dice tomatoes, avocados and green onions. Take cooled refried beans and salsa and spread in 11 x 13-inch pan. Spread sour cream/taco seasoning mixture over beans.

Layer the cheese, olives, lettuce, tomatoes, avocados and green onion in above order evenly over each ingredient. Serve with tortilla chips.

Yield: 8 servings

FITNESS FACT – An exercise program that includes regular strength training can take up to 20 years off our fitness age in as little as a year!

Fruit Salsa and Cinnamon Chips

2   kiwis, peeled and diced

2   Golden Delicious apples –
      peeled, cored and diced

8   ounces raspberries

1   pound strawberries

2   tablespoons white sugar

1   tablespoon brown sugar

3   tablespoons fruit preserves, any
      flavor

10   (10-inch) flour tortillas
      Butter flavored cooking spray

2   cups cinnamon sugar

In a large bowl, thoroughly mix kiwis, Golden Delicious apples, raspberries, strawberries, white sugar, brown sugar and fruit preserves. Cover and chill in refrigerator at least 15 minutes.

Preheat oven to 350 degrees.

Coat one side of each flour tortilla with butter flavored cooking spray. Cut into wedges and arrange in a single layer on a larger cookie sheets. Sprinkle wedges with desired amount of cinnamon sugar. Spray again with cooking spray.

Bake 8-10 minutes. Repeat with any remaining tortilla wedges. Allow to cool about 15 minutes. Serve with chilled fruit and spice mixture.

Yield: 10 servings

ACTIVITY – <u>Kleinhans Music Hall, Buffalo (Erie)</u> – built in the shape of a violin or cello, is home to the famous Buffalo Philharmonic Orchestra.

Chunky Guacamole

3	medium-sized, ripe avocados
2	tablespoons minced onion
1	medium garlic clove, minced
1	small jalapeño chile, minced (1 to 1½ teaspoons)
¼	cup minced fresh cilantro leaves
¼	teaspoon salt
½	teaspoon ground cumin (optional)
2	tablespoons juice of 1 lime

To minimize the risk of discoloration; prepare the minced ingredients first so they are ready to mix with the avocados as soon as they are cut.

Half one avocado, remove pit, and scoop flesh into medium bowl. Mash flesh lightly with onion, garlic, jalapeño, cilantro, salt, and cumin (if using) with tines of a fork until just combined.

Half and pit remaining two avocados. Gently scoop out avocado into bowl with mashed avocado mixture. To half avocado: Use dish towel to hold avocado steady. Make ½-inch cross-hatch incisions in flesh with a dinner knife, cutting down to but not through skin. Separate diced flesh from skin using spoon inserted between skin and flesh, gently scooping out avocado cubes.

Sprinkle juice of 1 lime over diced avocado and mix entire contents of bowl lightly with fork until combined but still chunky. Adjust seasoning with salt, if necessary, and serve. (Can be covered with plastic wrap, pressed directly onto surface of mixture, and refrigerated up to one day. Return guacamole to room temperature, removing plastic wrap at the last moment, before serving.)

Yield: 2½-3 cups

FUN FACT – Avocados have the highest calories of any fruit at 167 calories per hundred grams.

Spinach Balls

¼	cup melted butter
2	eggs
1	(8-ounce) package frozen chopped spinach, thawed and drained
1	medium onion, chopped
¼	cup grated Parmesan or Romano cheese or combination of both
¼	teaspoon garlic
¼	teaspoon salt
1	cup seasoned bread crumbs

Preheat oven to 350 degrees.

Over medium heat, melt butter. In large mixing bowl lightly beat eggs and melted butter. Add spinach, onion, cheese, garlic, salt and bread crumbs. Mix thoroughly and refrigerate at least 8 hours.

Roll mixture into 1-1½-inch balls and place on cookie sheet. Bake about 15-20 minutes or until browned. Serve at once.

ACTIVITY – Chestnut Ridge Park, Orchard Park (Erie) – The oldest of county parks offers unique features of hiking trails, a ravine, and the Eternal Flame Falls Waterfall. At the base of the waterfall is a small grotto with natural gas jets escaping through the cracks, igniting into small flames.

Mixed Bean Pâté

14	ounces mixed beans (drained and without added sugar or salt if beans are from a can)
2	tablespoons olive oil
1	lemon, juice only
2	garlic cloves, finely chopped
1	tablespoon fresh cilantro, chopped
2	green onions, chopped
	Salt and pepper to taste
	Shredded green onions, for garnish

Rinse beans thoroughly under cold running water and drain well. Transfer beans to a food processor or blender and process until smooth or place beans in a bowl and mash with a fork or potato masher.

Add olive oil, lemon juice, garlic, cilantro and green onions; blend until fairly smooth. Season with salt and pepper to taste.

Transfer to serving bowl and chill for at least 30 minutes, garnish with green onions.

Serve with baguettes or crackers.

FITNESS FACT – Lack of physical activity is a risk factor for heart disease.

White and Bleu Beer Fondue

1	pound bleu cheese, crumbled
1	pound sharp white Cheddar cheese
2	cups beer (avoid dark colored beers)
	Salt and pepper to taste
1	French bread
1	apple
1	pear
1	teaspoon lemon juice
4-6	stalks asparagus

In a fondue pot or slow cooker melt bleu cheese, Cheddar cheese with beer. Add salt and pepper to taste.

Slice off about 6-inches of French bread and cut into 1-1½-inch cubes.

Cut apple and pear into 1-1½-inch cubes (peeling optional). In a small bowl gently toss apple and pear cubes with lemon juice until coated (lemon juice will keep the fruit from turning brown).

Snap off bottoms of asparagus stalks. In a pot boil about 2-inches of water, add asparagus to boiling water for 10-15 seconds remove and immediately run under cold water. This process is called blanching, which is used to remove skin from foods (e.g. tomatoes), set flavors before freezing foods or enhance color and flavor in foods such as asparagus. After briefly boiling the food the cold water stops the cooking process.

Serve bread, fruit and asparagus on plate with skewers or long fork for dipping.

ACTIVITY – Buffalo & Erie County Botanical Gardens, Buffalo (Erie) – Three historic attractions: 1899 tri-domed glass conservatory, Olmstead's South Park and the Victorian style gardens.

Sesame, Lemon and Curry Chicken Strips

½ cup plain low-fat yogurt

⅓ cup purchased mango chutney

2 tablespoons chopped fresh cilantro

4 boneless skinless chicken breast halves

½ cup fresh lemon juice

¾ cup sesame seeds

4 large garlic cloves, minced

4 teaspoons curry powder

Salt and pepper to taste

Blend yogurt and chutney in processor. Add cilantro and process 5 seconds.

Transfer sauce to small bowl. (Can be prepared 1 day ahead. Cover and chill.)

Arrange chicken in shallow dish. Pour lemon juice over. Refrigerate at least 15 minutes and up to 30 minutes, turning chicken occasionally.

Preheat oven to 400 degrees. Lightly grease cookie sheet. Drain chicken. Combine sesame seeds and garlic in shallow bowl. Sprinkle both sides of chicken with curry powder. Season with salt and pepper. Press chicken into sesame seed and garlic mixture, coating completely. Arrange chicken on prepared sheet. Bake chicken about 20 minutes until just cooked through. Let stand 15 minutes. Cut chicken crosswise into ½-inch wide strips.

Arrange chicken strips around edge of serving platter. Place chutney dip in center and serve.

FUN FACT – Cilantro is also called coriander, Chinese parsley and Mexican parsley. It is used as a main ingredient in Mexican salsa. Also good with fish, chicken and pork.

Bacon and Tomato Cups

8	slices bacon
1	tomato, chopped
½	onion, chopped
3	ounces shredded Swiss cheese
½	cup mayonnaise
1	teaspoon dried basil
1	(16-ounce) can refrigerated buttermilk biscuit dough

Preheat oven to 375 degrees. Lightly grease a mini muffin pan.

In a skillet over medium heat, cook bacon until evenly brown. Drain on paper towels. Crumble bacon into a medium mixing bowl, and mix with tomato, onion, Swiss cheese, mayonnaise and basil.

Separate biscuits into halves horizontally. Place each half into cups of the prepared mini muffin pan. Fill each biscuit half with the bacon mixture.

Bake 10-12 minutes or until golden brown.

Yield: 15 servings

ACTIVITY – Buffalo St. Patrick's Day Parade, Buffalo (Erie) – In Ireland this may be a quiet day of reverence for Saint Patrick, but in Buffalo it is a day of wearing the green. Thousands flock to downtown Buffalo where every light pole along the parade route is decorated with the American flag and the tri-colored flag of Ireland – rain, snow or shine.

Carrot Soup

6   carrots, medium to large size, chopped
1   medium onion, sliced
3   medium potatoes, cubed
2   quarts water
4   slices bacon
2   tablespoons butter
     Salt and pepper to taste

In a large pot, combine vegetables and water. Cook covered until vegetable are tender. In a small skillet, cook bacon until crispy, let cool and chop or crumble into small pieces. Add bacon, butter and season with salt and pepper to taste. Simmer 10 minutes and serve.

Yield: 8 servings

FUN FACTS – Carrots Really Can Help You See In The Dark! Vitamin A is known to prevent "night blindness", and carrots are loaded with Vitamin A.

Zucchini and Rosemary Soup

2	tablespoons (¼ stick) butter
1	tablespoon vegetable oil
1	large onion, chopped
2	garlic cloves, sliced
2	teaspoons minced fresh rosemary
6	cups chicken broth or canned low-salt broth
1	russet potato, peeled, sliced
3	medium zucchini, thinly sliced
	Salt
	Ground pepper
1	zucchini, cut into ½-inch cubes
	Croutons
	Chopped green onions

Melt butter with oil in heavy large saucepan over medium-high heat. Add onion; sauté until translucent, about 5 minutes. Mix in garlic and rosemary. Add broth and potato; bring to boil. Reduce heat and simmer 10 minutes. Add sliced zucchini; simmer until tender about 15 minutes. Working in batches, purée in blender. Season with salt and pepper.

Cook cubed zucchini in saucepan of boiling salted water for 30 seconds. Drain. Reheat soup over medium heat. Ladle into bowls. Top with zucchini and croutons.

Sprinkle with green onions.

Yield: 8 servings

ACTIVITY – <u>Cave of the Winds, Goat Island (Niagara)</u> – Wear rain gear provided by the tour while walking under the Bridal Falls and experience the force, noise and spray of the Falls.

Bisque of Mushroom Soup

4	cups mushrooms
1	medium onion, chopped
2	cups vegetable stock or water
7	tablespoons butter or margarine
6	tablespoons plain flour
2	cups milk
1	cup heavy cream
	Salt and pepper to taste
	Chopped chives for garnish

Set aside four whole mushrooms and finely chop the remaining. In a saucepan, combine the onion chopped mushrooms and vegetable stock. Cover and simmer for 30 minutes.

Slice the 4 remaining mushrooms and sauté with 1 tablespoon butter until browned. Melt the remaining butter in a large pot and slowly whisk in flour into the butter until smooth. Add milk and whisk constantly, bringing to a boil. Reduce heat and simmer for 2-3 minutes.

Add the mushroom and stock mixture, sautéed mushrooms and cream. Stir until thoroughly combined. Season to taste with salt and pepper. Pour into bowls, garnish with chives and serve immediately.

Yield: 6-8 servings

ACTIVITY – Roger Tory Peterson Institute, Jamestown (Chautauqua) – This natural history institute has hosted many traveling exhibits of wildlife art and photography.

Beet and Potato Salad

4	beets, topped and tailed
3	medium white potatoes
6	garlic cloves, minced
3	tablespoons olive oil
	Juice of 1 lemon

Chop and steam beet tops (greens) and tails. Drain and cool. Simmer beets until tender. Drain and cool. When cooled, slip off skins.

Cook potatoes in jackets until tender when poked with a fork. Drain, cool, and peel.

Cube beets and potatoes and place in bowl with greens.

Dressing: Whisk garlic with oil and lemon juice. Season dressing to taste, then toss with beets and potatoes. Serve chilled with crusty bread.

ACTIVITY – The Reinstein Woods Nature Preserve in Depew (Erie) – contains 80 acres of forest which has remained much the same for centuries.

Celery & Cheese Salad

1 cup chopped celery
1 cup peas, frozen
1 carrot, grated
1 teaspoon grated onion
½ cup mayonnaise
1 cup shredded Cheddar cheese
Salt and pepper
Lettuce leaves

Toss together celery, peas, carrot, and onion. Add mayonnaise. Fold in shredded cheese and season to taste. Serve on crisp lettuce.

FUN FACTS – Hydroponics is the technique by which plants are grown in water without soil.

Broccoli and Cherry Tomato Salad

4	cups broccoli florets
1	pint basket cherry tomatoes, halved
2	teaspoons Dijon mustard
3	tablespoons seasoned rice vinegar
1	tablespoon olive oil
2	tablespoons chopped fresh oregano, or 2 teaspoons dried

Steam broccoli until just crisp-tender, about 4 minutes. Dip broccoli in ice-water to stop cooking and retain bright green color. Remove and drain. Transfer to large bowl and cool. Add tomatoes.

Place mustard in a small bowl. Gradually whisk in vinegar, then oil. Mix in oregano.

Add to salad and toss to coat. Season with salt and pepper. Refrigerate until serving.

Yield: 6 servings

ACTIVITY – <u>The Underground Railroad Tour</u> begins in Buffalo and crosses to the Canadian side of the Niagara River. Harriett Tubman used the "Freedom Crossing" at the lower Niagara gorge. No bridges existed at that time.

Lemon-Lime Soda Salad

1	(6-ounce) package lemon gelatin
1	cup hot water
1	cup lemon-lime soda
2	cups crushed pineapple in juice, juice reserved
3	bananas, diced
½	cup sugar
2	tablespoons flour
½	cup reserved pineapple juice
2	tablespoons butter
1	egg, beaten
1	cup heavy cream

Dissolve gelatin in hot water, then add lemon-lime soda. Chill until partly set. Add crushed pineapple and diced bananas: chill until firm.

Mix sugar and flour. Add reserved pineapple juice, butter and egg. Cook until thick over medium heat, stirring constantly. The egg in this makes it very easy to scorch. When thickened, allow to cool.

Whip the cream and fold into the cooked mixture. Spread on top of firmly set gelatin.

FITNESS FACT – You burn about the same number of calories doing 6 sessions, 5 minutes each, of an activity as doing 1 session of 30 minutes.

Cucumber and Red Onion Salad

2   cucumbers, peeled and sliced very thin

     Salt

1   cup cider vinegar

¼   cup sugar

½   red onion, cut in half and sliced thin

     Fresh dill, chopped

Place the cucumber slices in layers in a large colander, lightly salting each layer before starting the next. Place a large plate, weighted with a heavy object, on top of the layers of cucumbers.

Place the colander over a large bowl (to catch the drippings). Refrigerate.

Heat the vinegar, sugar and red onions in a saucepan over low heat until the sugar dissolves (2-3 minutes). Transfer to a serving bowl. Cool.

Remove the cucumbers from the refrigerator. Rinse thoroughly under cold water. Pat dry with paper towels. Add to the onion mixture.

Refrigerate, covered, for at least 3 hours (overnight is better). Drain the mixture, reserving 5 tablespoons. Toss the salad with the dressing.

Garnish with chopped dill. Serve.

ACTIVITY – The oldest state park in the United States is the Niagara Reservation State Park which surrounds Niagara Falls (Niagara). The trolley rides, observation tower (80 feet above ground and 180 feet down to the falls), and the Maid of the Mist Boats are famous attractions.

Zucchini Fiesta Salad

½ pound zucchini, cut crosswise in ¼-inch thick slices

½ pound yellow squash cut crosswise in ¼-inch thick slices

2 tablespoons lemon juice

¼ cup salad oil

Salt

Dash pepper

Dash ground cumin

1 green onion, thinly sliced

⅓ cup diced green chilies

⅓ cup pimento-stuffed olives, chopped

1 (3-ounce) package cream cheese, cubed

1 small avocado

Lettuce leaves

Fresh coriander (cilantro)

Steam zucchini and squash over boiling water until crisp-tender (about 3 minutes). Plunge into ice water to cool; drain well.

In a large bowl, combine lemon juice, oil, salt, pepper, and cumin. Add drained squash and stir lightly; chill for 30 minutes. Add onion, chilies, olives, and cheese. Peel and pit avocado, cut into small cubes. Add to salad and mix lightly.

To serve, arrange lettuce leaves on 4 salad plates. Mound equal portions of salad on each plate.

Garnish each salad with a sprig of coriander.

FUN FACTS – Avocados are "fruits" that date back to the Aztecs. The Spaniards brought them to this country in the 1800's.

Honey Granola Bread

3½ cups all-purpose flour
2 packages (¼-ounce each) active dry yeast
1 teaspoon salt
1¾ cups fat-free milk
½ cup plus 2 tablespoons honey
5⅓ tablespoons butter or stick margarine
2 eggs
2 cups whole wheat flour
1 cup reduced-fat granola without raisins
1 cup rye flour
½ cup cornmeal
½ cup quick-cooking oats
¼ cup slivered almonds, toasted and chopped

In a large mixing bowl, combine 2 cups all-purpose flour, yeast and salt. In a saucepan, heat the milk, honey and butter to 120-130 degrees. Add to dry ingredients; beat just until moistened. Add eggs; beat until smooth. Stir in whole wheat flour and enough remaining all-purpose flour to form a soft dough (dough will be sticky). Stir in the granola, rye flour, cornmeal, oats and almonds.

Turn dough onto a floured surface; knead until smooth and elastic, about 6-8 minutes. Place in a greased bowl, turning once to grease top. Cover and let rise in a warm place until doubled, about 1 hour.

Punch dough down. Turn onto a floured surface. Divide in half; cover and let rest for 10 minutes. Shape each portion into a ball. Place on a greased baking sheet; flatten into 5-inch circles. Cover and let rise in a warm place until doubled, about 30 minutes. Bake at 375 degrees for 20 minutes; cover with foil. Bake 10 minutes longer or until bread sounds hollow when tapped. Remove to wire racks.

Yield: 2 loaves (16 slices each)

ACTIVITY – Zoar Valley in Cattaraugus County has some of the best hiking in Western New York.

Soda Bread

4	cups flour
1	teaspoon salt
1	teaspoon baking soda
1	teaspoon sugar (optional)
2	cups buttermilk

Mix dry ingredients. Add enough buttermilk to make a soft dough. Knead the dough lightly. Form a round loaf about as thick as your fist. Place it on a lightly-floured baking sheet and cut a cross in the top with a floured knife. Bake near the top of a preheated 450 degree oven for 30-45 minutes.

FUN FACT – The Word "Salary" Comes From "Salt!". Salt, our oldest preservative, was extremely rare in the past. So rare, that is was often used as pay. Today, salt is so common that restaurants give it away for free, and packaged food contains so much that it's far too easy to eat too much salt, which is also known as sodium.

Herbed Vegetable Spiral Bread

½ cup shredded part-skim
    mozzarella cheese
½ cup canned Mexicorn, drained
¼ cup grated Parmesan cheese
¼ cup minced fresh parsley
2 garlic cloves, minced
1 teaspoon dried oregano
½ teaspoon dried basil
½ teaspoon ground cumin
¼ teaspoon salt
⅛-¼ teaspoon crushed red pepper
    flakes, optional
1 (1 pound) loaf frozen bread
    dough, thawed
1 tablespoon cornmeal
1 egg, lightly beaten

In a bowl, combine the mozzarella, corn, Parmesan, parsley, garlic and seasonings; set aside. On a lightly floured surface, roll dough into a 16 x 12-inch rectangle. Spread cheese mixture over dough to within ¾-inch of edges. Roll up jelly-roll style, starting with a long side; pinch seams and ends to seal. Sprinkle a large baking sheet with cornmeal. Place dough seam side down on baking sheet; tuck ends under. Cover and let rise in a warm place until doubled, about 35 minutes.

Brush with egg. Bake at 350 degrees for 35-40 minutes or until golden brown and bread sounds hollow when tapped. Cool for 20 minutes before slicing. Store leftovers in the refrigerator.

Yield: 16 slices

ACTIVITY – <u>Antiquing</u> – Set out for a search of that "one of a kind" or a trip down memory lane.

Carrot Cake Muffins

2	cups all-purpose flour
2	teaspoons baking soda
2	teaspoons cinnamon
¼	teaspoon salt
1¼	cups sugar
¼	pound carrots
½	cup pecans
½	cup raisins
¼	cup sweetened flaked coconut
3	large eggs
1	cup corn oil
2	teaspoons vanilla
1	Granny Smith apple

Preheat oven to 350 degrees and oil 18 (½-cup) muffin cups. In a large bowl sift together flour, baking soda, cinnamon, and salt. Whisk in sugar. Coarsely shred enough carrots to measure 2 cups and chop pecans. Add shredded carrots and pecans to flour mixture with raisins and coconut and toss well.

In a bowl whisk together eggs, oil*, and vanilla. Peel and core apple and coarsely shred. Stir shredded apple into egg mixture and add to flour mixture, stirring until batter is just combined well.

Divide batter among muffin cups, filling them three-fourths full, and bake in middle of oven until puffed and a tester comes out clean, 15-20 minutes. Cool muffins in cups on racks 5 minutes before turning out onto racks to cool completely. Muffins keep in an airtight container at room temperature 5 days.

To cut down on the oil, use ⅓ cup applesauce and ⅔ cup oil instead.

Yield: 18 muffins

FUN FACT – Vanilla is the extract of fermented and dried pods of several species of orchids.

Beverly's Calzones with Roasted Vegetables

2	bell peppers (medium)
1	onion (large)
4	portobello mushrooms
2	cups cooked spinach (optional)
½-⅔	cup olive oil
1	tablespoon Italian seasonings (other seasonings to taste)
2-4	cups 1½ to 2 cups pizza or spaghetti sauce
	Extra sauce
16	ounces shredded mozzarella cheese
1	pound pizza dough

Oven for roasting vegetables: 425 degrees. Oven for cooking calzones: 375 degrees.

Thaw pizza dough to room temperature.

Slice peppers, onion, and mushrooms into long strips. Put in large mixing bowl. Add olive oil and Italian seasonings. Mix well. Spread on large cookie sheet. Bake in preheated 425 degree oven for 15-20 minutes – until vegetables are just cooked. Remove from oven and set aside to cool.

Divide dough into two. Roll out ½ dough so it is a large rectangle - about 9 x 14-inch. Spread ½ of the sauce on the dough. Spread ½ of the roasted vegetables evenly on top of sauce. Add 1 cup of the spinach (optional). Sprinkle on 8-ounces of cheese. Carefully roll the dough from the narrow end, keeping the contents inside. Pinch the ends of the dough to help prevent leakage. Repeat above with the other half of the dough.

Place both calzones on a sprayed cookie sheet. Bake in preheated 375 degree oven for 25 minutes or until done. Heat extra sauce and serve as a topping for the calzones. Each calzone serves two people.

ACTIVITY – Bergen Swamp, Byron (Genesee) – A national natural history landmark with 1900 acres of rare and endangered species. Birding enthusiasts will enjoy the selection of "northern breeders". Visits to the swamp must be prearranged.

Black Bean Enchiladas

1	large onion, chopped
1	medium-sized green pepper, chopped
2	tablespoons chicken or vegetable broth
2	cans (15-ounce each) black beans, rinsed and drained, divided
1½	cups picante sauce, divided
12	(6-inch) flour tortillas
2	medium tomatoes, chopped
½	cup shredded reduced-fat Cheddar cheese
½	cup shredded part-skim mozzarella cheese
3	cups shredded lettuce
6	tablespoons fat-free sour cream

In a nonstick skillet, cook and stir onion and green pepper in broth for 2-3 minutes or until tender. Mash one can of black beans. Add to skillet with three-fourths cup picante sauce and remaining beans; heat through.

Spoon one-fourth cup mixture down the center of each tortilla. Roll up and place, seam side down, in a 13 x 9 x 2-inch baking dish coated with nonstick cooking spray. Combine tomatoes and remaining picante sauce; spoon over enchiladas.

Cover and bake at 350 degrees for 15 minutes. Uncover; sprinkle with cheeses. Bake 5 minutes longer. To serve, place one-half cup lettuce on each plate and top with two enchiladas. Garnish each serving with 1 tablespoon sour cream.

Yield: 6 servings

One serving (2 enchiladas) equals 404 calories, 9 grams fat (1 gram saturated), 7 milligrams cholesterol, 1,477 milligrams sodium, 60 grams carbohydrate, 9 grams fiber, 21 grams protein. Diabetic Exchanges: 3 lean meat, 2½ starch, 1 fat.

FITNESS FACT – The key to successful exercise program is choosing an activity that you will enjoy. Even moderate levels of activity have important health benefits.

Scallops and Asparagus Stir-Fry

¾ pound fresh asparagus, trimmed and cut into 2-inch pieces
1 tablespoon cornstarch
¾ cup chicken broth
1 teaspoon reduced-sodium soy sauce
¾ pound sea scallops, halved
1 cup sliced fresh mushrooms
1 garlic clove, minced
2 teaspoons canola oil
1 cup halved cherry tomatoes
2 green onions, sliced
1 teaspoon sesame oil
⅛ teaspoon pepper
2 cups hot cooked rice

Place asparagus in a saucepan and cover with water; bring to boil. Cook, uncovered, for 3-5 minutes or until crisp-tender; drain and set aside. In a small bowl, combine the cornstarch, broth and soy sauce until smooth; set aside.

In a large nonstick skillet or wok, stir-fry scallops, mushrooms and garlic in canola oil until scallops are opaque and mushrooms are tender. Stir cornstarch mixture; add to skillet. Bring to boil; cook and stir until sauce is thickened. Add the tomato, onion, sesame oil, pepper and reserved asparagus; heat through. Serve over rice.

Yield: 4 servings

One serving (1 cup stir-fry mixture with ½ cup rice) equals 215 calories, 5 gram fat (1 gram saturated fat), 14 milligrams cholesterol, 314 milligrams sodium, 30 grams carbohydrate, 2 grams fiber, 11 grams protein. Diabetic Exchanges: 1½ starch, 1 vegetable, 1 lean meat, ½ fat.

ACTIVITY – Beaver Meadow Audubon Center, Java (Wyoming) – a 324 acre sanctuary and nature center with 8 miles of trails. Beavers, which were nearly extinct in Western New York by the 1940's, now thrive in the pond and surrounding area. The center also features the Buffalo Astronomical Association's observatory.

Basil Shrimp Fettuccine

8	ounces uncooked fettuccine
½	cup chopped onion
¼	cup each chopped sweet red pepper and yellow pepper
1-2	garlic cloves, minced
2	tablespoons olive or canola oil
¼	cup all-purpose flour
1	(12-ounce) can fat-free evaporated milk
½	teaspoon salt
¼	teaspoon white pepper
⅛	teaspoon cayenne pepper
1	pound uncooked shrimp, peeled and deveined
2	tablespoons minced fresh basil or 2 teaspoons dried basil

Cook pasta according to package directions. In a nonstick skillet, sauté onion, peppers, and garlic in oil until tender. In a small bowl, combine flour and milk until smooth. Add to vegetable mixture. Stir in seasonings. Bring to boil; cook and stir for 2 minutes or until thickened.

Reduce heat; add shrimp and basil. Simmer, uncovered, for 3 minutes or until shrimp turn pink. Drain pasta; place in large bowl. Add shrimp mixture and toss to coat.

Yield: 6 servings

One serving (1¼ cups) equals 306 calories, 7 grams fat (1 gram saturated fat), 115 milligrams cholesterol, 465 milligrams sodium, 37 grams carbohydrate, 2 grams fiber, 24 grams protein. Diabetic Exchanges: 2 starch, 2 lean meat, 1 fat.

FUN FACT – Sweet Basil is fragrant with underlying flavors of anise and clove. A natural with tomatoes. Add torn leaves to salads, use on vegetables, fish and in soups.

Opal Basil has deep purple leaves that taste like sweet basil. It can be used on vegetables, fish, and in soups.

Moist 'N' Tender Buffalo Wings

25   whole chicken wings
      (about 5 pounds)
1   (12-ounce) bottle chili sauce
¼   cup lemon juice
¼   cup molasses
2   tablespoons Worcestershire
      sauce
6   garlic cloves, minced
1   tablespoon chili powder
1   tablespoon salsa
1   teaspoon garlic salt
3   drops hot pepper sauce

Cut chicken wings into three sections; discard wing tips. Place the wings in a 5-quart slow cooker. In a bowl, combine the remaining ingredients; pour over chicken. Stir to coat. Cover and cook on low for 8 hours or until chicken is tender.

Yield: about 4 dozen

ACTIVITY – <u>Old Fort Niagara, Youngstown (Niagara)</u> – Old Fort Niagara Lighthouse is at the mouth of the Niagara River and Lake Ontario on the grounds of Old Fort Niagara State Park. There are three lighthouses in this location, two being lights that sat atop buildings inside the fort grounds.

Rosemary Lime Chicken

4	(5-ounce each) boneless skinless chicken breast halves
2	tablespoons canola oil
½	cup white wine or chicken broth
¼	cup lime juice
2	tablespoons fresh rosemary, minced or 2 teaspoons dried rosemary, crushed
½	teaspoon salt
¼	teaspoon pepper

Flatten chicken to ½-inch thickness. In a large skillet, brown chicken in oil over medium-high heat. Add the remaining ingredients. Cook, uncovered, for 5-7 minutes or until chicken juices run clear.

Yield: 4 servings

One serving equals 244 calories, 9 grams fat (1 gram saturated fat), 82 milligrams cholesterol, 389 milligrams sodium, 2 grams carbohydrate, trace fiber, 33 grams protein. Diabetic Exchanges: 4 lean meat, ½ fat.

FUN FACT – Rosemary is strong and distinctive with a piney scent. Often paired with poultry and meats. A natural complement to lamb. A winner with roasted potatoes and in marinades for grilled eggplant and peppers.

Roasted Asparagus with Balsamic Vinegar

1½   pounds fresh asparagus, trimmed
2   teaspoons olive or canola oil
½   teaspoon salt
⅛   teaspoon white pepper
3   tablespoons balsamic vinegar

Place the asparagus in a 13 x 9 x 2-inch baking dish. Sprinkle with oil, salt and pepper; toss to coat. Bake, uncovered at 425 degrees for 10-15 minutes or until lightly browned. Drizzle with vinegar just before serving.

Yield: 4 servings

Carrot Raisin Pilaf

1   medium onion, chopped
2   tablespoons butter or stick margarine
2½   cups water
2   medium carrots cut into 1-inch julienne strips
1   cup uncooked long grain rice
½   cup raisins
1   tablespoon chicken bouillon granules
½   teaspoon curry powder
¼   teaspoon salt
¼   teaspoon dried thyme
¼   cup slivered almonds, toasted

In a saucepan, sauté onion in butter until tender. Stir in water and next 7 ingredients. Bring to boil. Reduce heat; cover and simmer 15-20 minutes or until rice is tender. Sprinkle with almonds before serving.

Yield: 6 servings

ACTIVITY – Nannen Arboretum, Ellicottville (Cattaraugus) – The only arboretum in Western New York, 8 acres with hundreds of species of trees, herbs, shrubs and flowers.

Savory Lemon Limas

½ cup water
1 (10-ounce) package frozen lima beans
1 tablespoon butter or stick margarine, melted
1 tablespoon lemon juice
1 teaspoon sugar
½-¾ teaspoon ground mustard
¼ teaspoon salt

In a saucepan, bring water to boil. Add lima beans; return to boil. Reduce heat; cover and simmer 8-10 minutes or until tender. Drain. Combine butter, lemon juice, sugar, mustard and salt; pour over beans and toss to coat.

Yield: 4 servings

Tangy Green Beans

1½ pounds fresh green beans, trimmed
⅓ cup diced sweet red pepper
4½ teaspoons olive or canola oil
4½ teaspoons water
1½ teaspoons white wine vinegar or cider vinegar
1½ teaspoons spicy brown mustard
¾ teaspoon salt
¼ teaspoon pepper
⅛ teaspoon garlic powder

Place beans and sweet red pepper in a basket over 1-inch of boiling water in a saucepan. Cover and steam 7-8 minutes or until crisp-tender. In a bowl, whisk together the remaining ingredients. Transfer bean mixture to a serving bowl; add vinaigrette and stir to coat.

Yield: 9 servings

FITNESS FACT – Exercise helps you feel better, look good, and can improve your overall sense of well being. It can increase your physical strength and stamina. Proper exercise also can improve your circulation and the performance of your heart and lungs.

Southwest Skillet Corn

1	medium sweet red pepper, chopped
1	tablespoon finely chopped seeded jalapeño pepper
1	tablespoon butter or stick margarine
1½	teaspoons ground cumin
1	(16-ounce) package frozen corn, thawed
⅓	cup minced fresh cilantro or parsley

In a large nonstick skillet, sauté red pepper and jalapeño in butter until tender. Add cumin; cook 30 seconds. Add corn and cilantro; sauté 2 minutes longer or until heated through.

Yield: 4 servings

Mashed Potato Timbales

2½	pounds potatoes, peeled and cubed
1	tablespoon butter or stick margarine
1	tablespoon grated onion
1	(8-ounce) carton reduced-fat ricotta cheese
1	(8-ounce) cup reduced-fat sour cream
1	teaspoon salt
1	teaspoon garlic powder
½	teaspoon dried rosemary, crushed
¼	teaspoon pepper
2	egg whites
2	tablespoons dry bread crumbs

Place potatoes in a saucepan and cover with water; bring to boil. Reduce heat; cover and cook 20-25 minutes or until tender. Drain. Mash potatoes with butter and onion until small lumps of potato remain; set aside. In a mixing bowl, beat ricotta cheese and next 5 ingredients until smooth. In a small bowl, beat egg whites until frothy; fold into cheese mixture. Fold into potato mixture.

Generously coat muffin cups with nonstick spray; evenly sprinkle muffin cups with bread crumbs. Fill with potato mixture; smooth tops. Bake, uncovered, at 425 degrees for 27-30 minutes or until edges of potatoes are lightly browned. Cool 15 minutes. Loosen timbales from sides of muffin cups; invert onto a cookie sheet to remove.

Yield: 12 servings

ACTIVITY – Dunn House, Hamburg (Erie) – Visit an historic house managed by the Hamburg Historical Society.

Sweet Potato Pancakes

1   pound sweet potatoes, peeled and shredded
2   green onions, chopped
2   eggs, slightly beaten
¼   cup all-purpose flour
½   teaspoon salt
½   teaspoon pepper
5   tablespoons reduced-fat sour cream
    Finely chopped sweet red pepper and sliced green onions, optional

In a bowl, combine sweet potatoes, onions, eggs, flour, salt and pepper; mix well. Drop batter by ¼ cupfuls onto cookie sheets coated with nonstick cooking spray; flatten slightly. Bake at 400 degrees for 8 minutes; turn pancakes over. Bake 8-10 minutes longer or until potatoes are tender and pancakes are golden brown. Top with sour cream; garnish with sweet red pepper and onions if desired.

Yield: 5 servings

FUN FACT – The 10 most recognized food characters are: Pillsbury Doughboy, 7-UP Spot, California Raisins, M&M Characters, Tony The Tiger, Trix Rabbit, Nestle Quick Bunny, Ronald McDonald, Chester Cheetah (Frito-Lay), Elsie, The Borden Cow.

Strawberry Almond Cream Tart

Crust
36 honey graham crackers (about 9 sheets)
2   tablespoons sugar
2   tablespoons butter, melted
4   teaspoons water
    Cooking spray

Filling
⅔   cup light cream cheese
⅔   cup sugar
½   teaspoon vanilla extract
¼   teaspoon almond extract

Topping
6   cups small fresh strawberries, divided
⅔   cup sugar
1   tablespoon cornstarch
1   tablespoon fresh lemon juice
2   tablespoons sliced almonds, toasted

Preheat oven to 350 degrees.

To prepare crust, place crackers in a food processor; process until crumbly. Add 2 tablespoons sugar, butter, and water; pulse just until moist. Place in an 8 x 12-inch rectangular removable-bottom tart pan coated with cooking spray; press into bottom and ¾-inch up on sides of pan.

Bake for 10 minutes or until lightly browned. Cool on a wire rack.

To prepare filling, combine cream cheese and next 3 ingredients; stir until smooth. Spread over bottom of tart shell.

To prepare topping, place 2 cups strawberries in food processor; process until puréed. Combine strawberry purée, ⅔ cup sugar, and cornstarch in a small saucepan over medium heat, stirring constantly. Reduce heat to low; cook 1 minute. Remove glaze from heat, and cool to room temperature, stirring occasionally.

Combine 4 cups strawberries and juice; toss to coat. Arrange berries, bottoms up, in a rectangular pattern over filling. Spoon half of glaze evenly over berries (reserve remaining glaze for another use). Sprinkle nuts around edge. Cover and chill 3 hours.

Yield: 10 servings.

You can use either 9-inch round removable bottom tart pan or a 9-inch springform pan. The recipe also works with a 9-inch round tart pan or a 10-inch pie plate.

Calories 289 (28% from fat); fat 8.9g (sat 4.2g, mono 1.7g, poly 0.5g); protein 4.5g; CARB 48.7g; fiber 3g; cholesterol 15 mg; iron 1.3mg; sodium 242 mg; calcium 59mg

ACTIVITY – Originally built in 1839, the Busti Grist Mill is water turbine-powered. Visit the mill and the Historical Society Museum in Jamestown (Chautauqua).

Raspberry Custard Tart

Sauce

½	pint fresh raspberries
1	cup sugar
¼	cup water
1	tablespoon unsalted butter
⅛	teaspoon salt

Pastry

1⅓	cups all-purpose flour
¼	cup sugar
¼	teaspoon salt
1	stick cold unsalted butter
2	tablespoons heavy cream
1	large egg yolk
1½	tablespoons fresh lemon juice
1	teaspoon finely grated lemon zest

Filling

1	pint raspberries, plus more for serving
1½	cups heavy cream
4	large egg yolks
¼	cup sugar
1	vanilla bean, split and scraped

For Sauce: Purée raspberries in a food processor or blender. Strain purée through a fine sieve set over a medium bowl and discard the solids. In a small heavy saucepan, bring sugar and water to a boil. Cook over moderately high heat, without stirring, until a medium-amber caramel forms, about 6 minutes. Reduce heat to low and carefully stir in raspberry purée until smooth. Stir in butter, remove from heat and stir in salt. Let raspberry sauce cool completely.

For Pastry: In a food processor, pulse the flour with the sugar and salt. Cut the butter into 8 pieces and add to the flour; pulse until the mixture resembles coarse meal. In a small bowl, whisk the cream with the egg yolk, lemon juice and zest. Add to the flour mixture and process just until large clumps of dough form. Pat the dough into a disk, wrap in plastic and chill until firm, about 30 minutes.

On a lightly floured surface, roll the dough ⅛-inch thick and fit in a 10-inch fluted tart pan with a removable bottom. Freeze 15 minutes, or until firm.

Preheat the oven to 350 degrees. Line the dough with foil and fill with pie weights or dried beans. Bake the tart shell for 25 minutes, then remove the foil and weights and bake for 5 minutes longer, or until the pastry is lightly browned on the bottom. Cover the shell loosely with foil if the sides begin to brown too quickly. Let cool completely on a rack.

For Filling: Arrange the raspberries in concentric circles over the bottom of the tart shell. In a small bowl, whisk the cream with the egg yolks, sugar and scraped vanilla seeds. Pour the custard into the tart shell. Bake in the middle of the oven for 50-55 minutes, or until the custard is set. Let the tart cool on a wire rack for at least 30 minutes. Serve with fresh raspberries and the raspberry-caramel sauce.

The sauce can be refrigerated for 2 weeks. Bring to room temperature before serving.

ACTIVITY – Erie County Fair and Expo, Hamburg (Erie) – The largest independent county fair in the nation lasts 11 days set on 265 acres. Established in 1819 as a one day fair in Buffalo, was moved to Hamburg in 1868. The fair features livestock, rides, entertainment and demonstrations.

Banana Cream Pie

Pastry

1¼	cups all-purpose flour
2	tablespoons confectioners' sugar
⅛	teaspoon salt
1	stick unsalted butter, chilled
¼	cup heavy cream
1	teaspoon cider vinegar
3	tablespoons apricot preserves, melted and strained

Filling

2	cups milk
3	large egg yolks
½	teaspoon pure vanilla extract
¾	cup granulated sugar
2	tablespoons all-purpose flour
2	tablespoons cornstarch
	Pinch of salt
¼	teaspoon freshly grated nutmeg
2	tablespoons unsalted butter
3	tablespoons light rum
½	teaspoon unflavored gelatin
2	tablespoons cold water
1	cup heavy cream, chilled
2	tablespoons superfine sugar
3	ripe bananas, sliced ¼-inch thick
2	ounces chocolate curls

For Pastry: Preheat the oven to 400 degrees. In a food processor, pulse flour, confectioners' sugar and salt. Add butter; pulse until mixture resembles small peas. In a bowl, combine heavy cream and vinegar; pour over crumbs and pulse until moistened. On a floured surface, knead pastry 2-3 times, just until it comes together. Shape into a disk, wrap in plastic and chill for 30 minutes.

On a lightly floured surface, roll out pastry to a 12-inch round about ⅛-inch thick. Fit round into a 9-inch glass pie plate. Trim overhang to ½-inch and fold under; crimp decoratively. Refrigerate until chilled.

Prick crust with a fork, line pastry with foil and fill with dried beans or pie weights. Bake for about 25 minutes, or until set. Remove foil and beans. Press down any air bubbles and bake for about 8 minutes, until pastry is golden; transfer to a rack and brush bottom and sides with preserves. Let cool.

For Filling: In a bowl, mix ¼ cup of the milk, the egg yolks and vanilla. In a saucepan, combine the granulated sugar, flour, cornstarch, salt and nutmeg. Add the remaining 1¾ cups of milk and bring to a simmer, whisking constantly. Add butter and stir over moderate heat until thick and smooth, 2-3 minutes. Remove from heat and whisk about ½ into the egg mixture. Return mixture to saucepan and cook over moderately high heat, stirring constantly, until thickened, about 3 minutes. Strain through a fine sieve set over a bowl and add 2 tablespoons of the rum. Press a piece of wax paper on the custard; refrigerate until chilled.

In a small glass bowl, sprinkle the gelatin over the cold water; let stand until softened. Microwave on high until melted, 15 seconds; cool. In a bowl, beat cream with superfine sugar, the remaining 1 tablespoon of rum and melted gelatin until soft peaks form. Arrange bananas in overlapping layers on crust and pour custard on top. Tap pie on the counter so custard settles. Spread whipped cream on top, and using the back of a spoon, make deep swirls. Refrigerate until firm, 4 hours. Garnish with chocolate curls and serve.

Yield: One (9-inch) pie

FUN FACT – Americans eat more bananas than any other fruit: a total of 11 billion a year.

Blueberry Lemon Tarts

1	cup graham cracker crumbs
1½	tablespoons granulated sugar
8	tablespoons unsalted butter, melted
2	tablespoons packed light brown sugar
¼	cup sour cream
¼	teaspoon vanilla
4	ounces cream cheese, softened
½	teaspoon finely grated fresh lemon zest
1⅓	cups blueberries (6-ounces)
	Confectioners' sugar for dusting

Preheat oven to 350 degrees with a baking sheet on middle rack.

Stir together graham cracker crumbs, granulated sugar, and butter in a bowl with a fork until combined well, then press mixture with your fingers and back of a spoon evenly and firmly onto bottom and up side of each tart pan. (If using ramekins, press mixture ¾-inch up sides.)

Put tart pans on preheated baking sheet and bake crusts until slightly darker, about 10 minutes, then cool 10 minutes on a rack. (Ramekins will need to cool an additional 5 minutes in refrigerator.) Gently push bottom of each tart pan to loosen crust, and then invert crust onto your hand and place on a serving plate. (If using ramekins, leave crusts in ramekins.)

While crusts cool, whisk together brown sugar, sour cream, and vanilla in a small bowl until sugar is dissolved. Beat cream cheese in a medium bowl with an electric mixer until smooth, then add sour cream mixture and zest, beating until just combined well.

Divide cream cheese filling among tart shells, spreading evenly, then top with blueberries and dust with confectioners' sugar.

Yield: 4 servings

Special equipment: 4 (3¾-inch) nonstick fluted tart pans or 4 (8-ounce) ramekins.

ACTIVITY – The Chautauqua Belle is an authentic sternwheeler steamboat ride where learning about 19th century nautical history is combined with a placid trip on the lake.

Christine's Poke Cake

1	package White or Yellow Cake Mix
1	package gelatin (desired flavor)
1	cup boiling water
½	cup cold water
1	(8-ounces) package whipped topping

Prepare cake as directed on box, using a 13 x 9-inch greased and floured baking pan.

Prepare gelatin in medium bowl by adding 1 cup of boiling water until powder is dissolved.

Add ½ cup of cold water.

When cake is done baking, let cake cool in the pan for 15 minutes.

Poke cake with a fork in ½-inch intervals. Spoon gelatin mixture over holes in the cake. Chill cake for at least 3-4 hours.

Top with whipped topping.

ACTIVITY – Lana's The Little House (Chautauqua) – Visit and tour this Storybook English Cottage complete with an English Garden…open year round.

Lite Peach Upside Down Cake

1	(15-ounces) can reduced sugar sliced peaches
2	tablespoons peach juice (reserved)
⅓	cup packed brown sugar
1	tablespoon butter or stick margarine, melted
¼	teaspoon ground cinnamon
⅛	teaspoon ground nutmeg
1½	cups all-purpose flour
⅔	cup sugar
¾	teaspoon baking powder
¼	teaspoon baking soda
¼	teaspoon salt
1	cup 1% buttermilk
1	egg
1	teaspoon vanilla extract
3	tablespoons butter or stick margarine, melted

Preheat oven to 350 degrees.

Drain peaches, reserve 2 tablespoons of the juice and pat the peaches dry. In a small bowl combine brown sugar, 1 tablespoon butter or stick margarine, cinnamon, nutmeg and reserved peach juice. Spread into a 9-inch baking pan coated with non-stick cooking spray. Cut peach slices in half lengthwise and arrange in a single layer over brown sugar mixture.

In a large bowl combine flour, sugar, baking powder, baking soda and salt. In medium bowl combine buttermilk, egg, vanilla and 3 tablespoons butter or stick margarine. Add to dry ingredients, stir until blended and spoon over peaches.

Bake until toothpick inserted near the center comes out clean, about 30-35 minutes.

Cool for 10 minutes before inverting on serving plate.

Serve warm.

Yield: 8 servings

Calories 273, 7 grams fat (4 saturated), 49 grams carbohydrates, 1 gram fiber, 4 grams protein

FITNESS FACT – Various studies have demonstrated that physical inactivity is a risk factor for heart disease.

Chocolate Cherry Torte

1 ½   cups pitted picked-over fresh tart cherries, halved (about 1 pint)
¾   cup sugar
1   tablespoon kirsch
¾   stick unsalted butter
3   large eggs
6   ounces fine-quality bittersweet chocolate (not unsweetened)
½   cup all-purpose flour
½   teaspoon salt
½   cup semi-sweet chocolate chips

Preheat oven to 325 degrees and butter and flour a 9-inch springform pan, knocking out excess flour.

In a bowl stir together cherries, one-quarter cup sugar, and kirsch and macerate 15 minutes.

Cut butter into pieces and separate eggs. Coarsely chop bittersweet chocolate and in a double boiler or a metal bowl set over a saucepan of barely simmering water melt chocolate with butter, stirring occasionally. Remove top of double boiler or bowl from heat and cool mixture slightly. Stir in yolks, flour, and salt until combined well. Gently stir in cherries and chocolate chips until just combined.

In a bowl with an electric mixer beat whites until they hold soft peaks and gradually add remaining one-half cup sugar, beating until whites just hold stiff glossy peaks. Stir half of whites into chocolate mixture to lighten and fold in remaining whites gently but thoroughly. Pour batter into pan and smooth top. Bake torte in middle of oven 50 minutes to 1 hour, or until a tester comes out with crumbs adhering.

Cool torte in pan on a rack (top will fall slightly and crack). Run a thin knife around edge of torte and remove side of pan. Torte may be made 1 day ahead and kept, loosely covered with plastic wrap, at cool room temperature.

Serve torte with lightly sweetened whipped cream.

This torte has a crisp top that shatters when cut and a fudgy tart cherry center.

ACTIVITY – <u>Buffalo Home & Garden Show, Buffalo (Erie)</u> – Hundreds of exhibits for indoor and outdoor homeowner projects, decorating ideas, building and landscaping.

Angel Food Cake

1½ cups large egg whites (10 to 11)
1   tablespoon warm water
1   cup sifted cake flour (not self-rising; sift before measuring)
1¼ cups superfine granulated sugar
1   tablespoon ground ginger (optional)
2   teaspoons vanilla
1   teaspoon cream of tartar
½   teaspoon salt

Preheat oven to 375 degrees.

Put whites and water in a very clean large metal bowl and swirl over simmering water or a gas flame until barely warm. Sift together flour, ¼ cup sugar, and ginger 4 times onto a sheet of wax paper.

Beat whites in standing electric mixer on medium speed until frothy. Add vanilla, cream of tartar, and salt. Increase speed to medium-high and beat just until soft peaks begin to form. Gradually beat in remaining cup sugar, 2 tablespoons at a time, occasionally scraping down side of bowl. Increase speed to high and beat until stiff, glossy peaks form. (Do not over beat.) Sift ⅓ of flour mixture over whites. Beat on low speed just until blended. Sift and beat in remaining flour in 2 more batches.

Gently pour batter into ungreased tube pan and smooth top. Run a rubber spatula or long knife through batter to eliminate any large air bubbles.

Bake cake in lower third of oven until golden and a tester comes out clean, about 40 minutes. Remove cake from oven and immediately invert pan. (If pan has "legs," stand it on those. Otherwise, place pan over neck of a bottle.) Cool cake completely, upside down. Turn pan right side up. Run a long, thin knife around outer edge of pan with a smooth motion. Do the same around center tube. Remove outer rim of pan and run knife under bottom of cake to release. Invert to release cake from tube, and invert again onto a serving plate.

Serve cake with whipped cream and berries.

Yield: 8 servings

FUN FACT – Egg whites will beat to a better volume if they're allowed to stand at room temperature for 20-30 minutes before whipping.

Lemon Bars

1½   cups all-purpose flour
½   cup powdered sugar
1½   sticks butter, cut into pieces, room
        temperature
4   eggs
1½   cups sugar
½   cup fresh lemon juice
1   tablespoon plus 1 teaspoon
        all-purpose flour
1   tablespoon grated lemon peel
        Powdered sugar

Preheat oven to 350 degrees.

Combine 1½ cups flour and ½ cup powdered sugar in large bowl. Add butter and cut in until mixture resembles coarse meal. Press mixture into bottom of 9 x 13 x 2-inch baking dish. Bake until golden brown, about 20 minutes. Remove from oven. Maintain oven temperature.

Beat eggs, 1½ cups sugar, lemon juice, 1 tablespoon plus 1 teaspoon flour and lemon peel in medium bowl to blend. Pour into crust. Bake until mixture is set, about 20 minutes. Cool. Cut into 24 bars. Sift powdered sugar over top before serving.

Yield: 24 servings

ACTIVITY – <u>Buffalo Niagara Guitar Festival, Buffalo (Erie)</u> – A nine day celebration of the guitar including classical jazz, blues, rock, country, fold and bluegrass, celebrity musicians and a guitar competition.

Cream Cheese Brownies

4   squares unsweetened chocolate
1½   sticks butter
2½   cups sugar
5   eggs
1¼   cups flour
1   (8-ounce) package cream cheese,
      softened

Read through this recipe entirely before you begin, as you will need to divide ingredients into separate batters in order to create two layers.

Preheat oven to 350 degrees. Grease a 13 x 9-inch aluminum foil baking pan.

Microwave together the chocolate and butter on high setting 2 minutes. Stir in 2 cups of the sugar and blend well. Stir in 4 eggs and 1 cup of flour. Spread this mixture in the greased pan.

Beat cream cheese, gradually adding remaining ingredients. Combine well.

Spoon second mixture over batter already in pan. Swirl together lightly stirring with knife to create a marble-like pattern. Bake in Preheated 350 degree oven for 40 minutes or until toothpick has grainy fudge bits but is not clean, like in a cake. Be careful not to overbake.

FUN FACT – Chocolate contains phenyl ethylamine (PEA), a natural substance that is reputed to stimulate the same reaction in the body as falling in love.

Chocolate Macaroon Squares

Hot Shortbread Base
1½	sticks unsalted butter
2	cups all-purpose flour
½	cup packed light brown sugar
½	teaspoon salt

Filling
4	large egg whites
1	cup sugar
1	teaspoon vanilla
½	cup all-purpose flour
2⅔	cups sweetened flaked coconut, (7-ounce) bag
1½	cups semi-sweet chocolate chips

Preheat oven to 350 degrees.

For Shortbread Base: Cut butter into ½-inch pieces. In a food processor process all ingredients until mixture begins to form small lumps. Sprinkle mixture into a 13 x 9 x 2-inch baking pan and with a metal spatula press evenly onto bottom. Bake shortbread in middle of oven until golden, about 20 minutes. While shortbread is baking, prepare topping.

For Filling: In a bowl whisk together whites, sugar, and vanilla until combined well and stir in flour and coconut. Sprinkle chocolate chips evenly over hot shortbread. Let chips melt and spread evenly over shortbread. Drop small spoonfuls of coconut mixture onto chocolate and with a fork spread evenly. Bake in middle of oven until top is golden, about 30 minutes. Cool completely in pan and cut into 24 bars. Bar cookies keep, covered, 5 days at room temperature.

Makes 24 bars

ACTIVITY – Niagara Climbing Center, North Tonawanda (Niagara) – offers indoor climbing and outdoor climbing on portable climbing walls.

Berry Cobbler

5	cups berries
1	cup sugar
3	tablespoons flour
3	tablespoons butter

Crust

2	cups all-purpose flour
2	tablespoons sugar
4	teaspoons baking powder
½	teaspoon salt
½	teaspoon cream of tartar
8	tablespoons butter
½	cup buttermilk

Preheat oven to 400 degrees.

Toss the fruit or berries with sugar and pour into a well grease 1½-quart oblong baking dish. Sprinkle about 3 tablespoons flour over the fruit and dot with butter. Set aside.

For Crust: Sift together into a bowl flour, sugar, baking powder, salt, and cream of tartar. Cut in the butter with a pastry blender or fork until the mixture resembled coarse meal. Add buttermilk, mix lightly and form dough into ball. Roll the dough out ¼-inch thick on a floured board. Cover fruit with the dough, trim edges. Cut a vent in the center of the dough, sprinkle extra sugar on top, if desired. Bake in a 400 degree oven about 40 minutes or until crust is golden brown. May be served warm or chilled.

FUN FACT – California's Frank Epperson invented the Popsicle in 1905 when he was 11-years old.

Berry Tiramisu

1	(12-ounce) package unsweetened frozen mixed berries
12	tablespoons sugar
1	(10-ounce) package frozen raspberries in syrup, thawed
¼	cup raspberry liqueur
3	(40-ounce) packages Champagne biscuits (4-inch-long ladyfinger-like biscuits)
3	(8-ounce) containers mascarpone cheese (see note)
2	teaspoons vanilla extract
1	(1-pint) basket strawberries, hulled
2	(½-pint) baskets raspberries
1	(½-pint) basket blueberries

Cook frozen mixed berries and 6 tablespoons sugar in heavy medium saucepan over medium heat until mixture resembles jam and is reduced to 1 cup, stirring frequently, about 15 minutes. Cool jam mixture.

Strain syrup from thawed raspberries through sieve set over bowl, pressing gently on solids. Discard solids. Add raspberry liqueur to raspberry syrup in bowl. Using sharp knife, trim 1 biscuit to 3-inch (about) length. Quickly dip biscuit into syrup, turning to coat lightly. Place rounded end up and sugared side against side of 9-inch-diameter springform pan with 2¾-inch-high sides. Repeat with as many biscuits as necessary to cover sides of pan. Dip more biscuits in syrup and arrange on bottom of pan, covering completely and trimming to fit.

In bowl, whisk mascarpone with 6 tablespoons sugar and vanilla to blend. Set aside. Thinly slice enough strawberries to measure ½ cup. Gently spread half of jam mixture over biscuits in bottom of pan. Spoon half of mascarpone mixture over; smooth top. Sprinkle with sliced strawberries, ½ cup fresh raspberries and ½ cup blueberries. Dip more biscuits into syrup; arrange over fruit in pan, covering completely and trimming to fit. Gently spread remaining jam mixture over biscuits. Spoon remaining mascarpone mixture over; smooth top. Cover; chill at least 4 hours or overnight.

Release pan sides. Transfer cake to platter. Arrange remaining fresh berries decoratively atop cake and serve.

Yield: 10 servings

Italian cream cheese available at Italian markets and specialty foods stores. If unavailable, blend 1½ pounds cream cheese with ½ cup whipping cream and 6 tablespoons sour cream. Use 3 cups for recipe.

ACTIVITY – Frank Lloyd Wright designed <u>Graycliff</u>, the summer retreat for the Darwin Martin family before World War II. The house sits on a cliff overlooking Lake Erie in <u>Derby</u>.

Granola

1	cup walnuts, broken into ¼ to ½-inch pieces
3	cups rolled oats
½	cup unsweetened shredded coconut
½	cup blanched almonds, halved
¼	cup sesame seeds
¼	cup sunflower seeds
¼	cup maple syrup
¼	cup honey
⅓	cup canola oil
1	cup raisins

Adjust oven rack to center position and heat oven to 325 degrees.

Mix first 6 ingredients together in large bowl. Heat maple syrup and honey together with oil in small saucepan, whisking occasionally, until warm. Pour mixture over dry ingredients; stir with spatula until mixture is thoroughly coated. Turn mixture onto an 11 x 17-inch jelly-roll pan, spreading into an even layer.

Bake, stirring and re-spreading mixture into an even layer every 5 minutes, until granola is light golden brown, about 15 minutes. Immediately turn granola onto another jelly-roll pan to stop cooking process. Stir in raisins, then spread granola evenly in pan set on a wire rack and cool at room temperature. Loosen dried granola with spatula; store in airtight container.

Yield: 7-8 cups

FITNESS FACT – Research suggest that drinking about two cups of fluid two hours before exercise and another six to eight ounces every 20 minutes can help optimize performance.

Autumn

Autumn

Nicole's Pumpkin Fritters

1   cup pumpkin purée
1   egg, slightly beaten
1   cup all-purpose flour
1   teaspoon baking powder
1   teaspoon curry powder
1   teaspoon salt
4   cups vegetable oil for frying

In a medium bowl, combine pumpkin, egg, flour, baking powder, curry powder and salt. Mix until smooth.

Heat oil in a deep saucepan to 325 degrees. Drop batter by spoonfuls into hot oil. Fry until golden brown, about 2 minutes. Remove with a slotted spoon and serve immediately.

Yield: 24 servings

ACTIVITY – Griffis Sculpture Park, Ashford Hollow (Cattaraugus) – over 100 giant metal sculptures set among 400 acres of woodlands, ponds and hiking trails. Kids are welcome to climb on the giant insects, a castle tower and maze, just to name a few.

Rosemary and Walnut Polenta

2½   cups canned low-salt chicken
      broth or vegetable broth
⅔   cup yellow cornmeal
¾   cup grated Gruyère cheese
3   tablespoons butter
⅓   cup walnuts, toasted, finely
      chopped
1½   teaspoons chopped fresh
      rosemary
8   walnut halves

Preheat oven to 350 degrees.

Butter 9-inch diameter glass pie dish. Bring broth to boil in heavy medium saucepan. Gradually whisk in cornmeal. Reduce heat to medium and whisk constantly until mixture thickens, about 6 minutes. Remove from heat. Add Gruyère cheese and 1½ tablespoons butter; stir until cheese melts. Stir in chopped walnuts and rosemary. Season with salt and pepper. Transfer polenta to prepared dish; using buttered knife, spread evenly. Cool until polenta is firm, at least 1 hour.

Line cookie sheet with foil. Cut polenta into 8 wedges. Transfer wedges, bottom side up, to prepared sheet. Dot wedges with 1½ tablespoons butter. Place 1 walnut half in center of each wedge. (Can be made 1 day ahead. Cover and chill.)

Bake about 12 minutes or until heated through.

Yield: 8 servings

FITNESS FACT – A pound of fat burns about 2 calories a day, but a pound of muscle burns up to 38 calories a day!

Broccoli Bites

3	tablespoons prepared Dijon mustard
4	tablespoons honey
2	cups broccoli florets
1	cup shredded Cheddar cheese
1	egg
1	cup milk
½	cup sifted all-purpose flour
½	teaspoon baking powder
½	teaspoon salt
½	teaspoon vegetable oil
½	cup vegetable oil for frying

To make the sauce, stir together the Dijon mustard and honey in a small bowl. Set aside.

Chop broccoli florets into small pieces or pulse lightly in food processor. Toss in a mixing bowl with shredded cheese. Set aside.

Beat egg and stir in milk. Sift flour, baking powder, and salt together and combine them with the egg and milk mixture, beating well. Beat in ½ teaspoon oil. Pour mixture over broccoli and Cheddar cheese and toss to coat well.

In a large skillet or saucepan heat oil to 375 degrees.

Drop broccoli mixture by spoonfuls into oil and fry until golden brown. Serve with honey mustard sauce.

Yield: Makes 2 dozen (12 servings)

ACTIVITY – Albright Knox Art Gallery, Buffalo (Erie) – Featuring modern and contemporary art, this museum was designed by E. B. Green in a classical Greek Architectural style. Select original artwork may be purchased, while Gallery members also have the option to rent the artwork for home or office. Founded in 1933, this was one of the first such rental/sale galleries to exist within a museum.

Renaissance Stuffed Mushrooms

12	large mushrooms
1	tablespoon olive oil
2	garlic cloves, peeled and minced
3	tablespoons chopped green onions
1	(8-ounce) package cream cheese, softened
3	tablespoons port wine
1	teaspoon Italian-style seasoning
¼	cup grated Parmesan cheese
¾	cup shredded Cheddar cheese
¼	teaspoon ground pepper
2	dashes hot pepper sauce

Preheat oven to 350 degrees.

Remove stems from mushrooms. Set aside caps. Finely chop stems, discarding hard pieces.

Heat olive oil in a medium saucepan over medium heat. Stir in mushroom caps, garlic and green onions. Cook and stir until soft, about 4 minutes. Remove from heat and allow to cool until easily handled.

In a medium bowl, mix together chopped mushroom stem pieces, cream cheese, port wine, Italian-style seasoning, Parmesan cheese, Cheddar cheese, ground pepper and hot pepper sauce.

Stuff mushroom caps with the mushroom stem mixture. Arrange on a medium cookie sheet and bake 20-25 minutes or until lightly browned.

Yield: 12 stuffed mushrooms (12 servings)

FUN FACT – Capsacin, which makes hot peppers "hot" to the human mouth, is best neutralized by casein, the main protein found in milk.

Goat Cheese and Honey Baguettes

1   (8-ounce) French-bread baguette
8   ounces soft fresh goat cheese
¼   cup honey
½   cup chopped toasted walnuts
½   tablespoon chopped fresh
       rosemary

Preheat oven to 350 degrees.

Cut eighteen ¼-inch diagonal slices from baguette. Spread goat cheese on each slice. Arrange in single layer on rimmed cookie sheet. Bake about 10 minutes or until edges are slightly golden and cheese softens.

Heat honey in small saucepan over medium heat until warm, about 2 minutes. Sprinkle toasts with walnut, then rosemary. Drizzle with honey and serve.

Yield: 18 servings

ACTIVITY – Pick your own apples at select orchards in Orleans, Chautauqua, Niagara, Genesee, and Erie counties. The most active ripening dates for apples are between September 1 and October 25 but can be picked as late as October 31 at some farms.

Stuffed Jalapeños with Cheese

1	(8-ounce) package cream cheese, room temperature and cut into 1-1½-inch cubes
1	(4-ounce) cup shredded reduced fat sharp Cheddar cheese
¼	cup fat-free mayonnaise
1	garlic clove, minced
½	teaspoon dried oregano
18	jalapeño peppers (about 3-inches long) halved lengthwise and seeds removed*
2	egg whites
1	tablespoon fat-free milk
1½	cups crushed corn flakes (place in sealed plastic bag and gently crush with your hand, do not over-crush or flakes will turn into powder)
	Cooking spray

Preheat oven to 350 degrees.

In a small mixing bowl combine cream cheese Cheddar cheese, mayonnaise, garlic and oregano and beat until blended. Pack equal amounts of mixture into pepper halves.

In a shallow bowl or dish whisk egg whites and milk until combined. Place crushed corn flakes in another shallow bowl or dish. Dip packed peppers into egg mixture (coating all sides); repeat with corn flakes.

Place stuffing side up on non-stick cookie sheet or cookie sheet coated with cooking spray. Bake about 30 minutes or until tops are browned. Serve immediately

Yield: 36 appetizers

Wear rubber or plastic gloves while cutting and seeding the jalapeños and do not touch your face.

Four appetizers 127 calories, 3 grams fat (2 grams saturated fat), 17 grams carbohydrates, 1 gram fiber, 10 grams protein

FITNESS FACT – Crash dieting can lead to muscle loss…and muscle loss slows down the metabolism. This is good news for hearty eaters!

Braised Eggplant and Peppers

4	tablespoons olive oil
1	(1-pound) unpeeled eggplant, cut into ¾-inch cubes
2	onions, halved, thinly sliced
5	garlic cloves, minced
2	sweet red peppers, cored, cut into ½-inch strips
1	teaspoon ground turmeric
1½	cups diced canned tomatoes with juices
½	teaspoon sugar
2	tablespoons fresh lemon juice
	Salt and pepper to taste
1	tablespoon chopped fresh cilantro

Heat 2 tablespoons olive oil in large nonstick skillet over medium-high heat. Add cubed eggplant and sauté until golden, about 5 minutes. Transfer eggplant to plate. Add remaining 2 tablespoons olive oil to same skillet and heat over medium-high heat. Add onions and garlic and sauté until onions are tender and golden, about 6 minutes.

Add bell peppers and ¾ teaspoon turmeric to skillet and sauté until peppers are almost tender, about 6 minutes.

Add tomatoes with their juices and sugar. Boil until mixture thickens slightly, about 5 minutes. Add eggplant; reduce heat and simmer until vegetables are tender, about 6 minutes longer. Stir in 2 tablespoons lemon juice. Season to taste with salt and pepper. Transfer to bowl and cool to room temperature. (Can be made up to 1 day ahead. Cover and refrigerate. Serve at room temperature.) Sprinkle with cilantro. Serve with fresh slices fresh bread or unseasoned crackers.

ACTIVITY – Evangola State Park, Irving (Erie) – preserves a stretch of Lake Erie shoreline 27 miles south of Buffalo. Features fishing, hiking, cross-country skiing, swimming, a campground and tranquil woods for the perfect escape.

Easy Artichoke Appetizers

2   (8-ounce) tubes of crescent rolls
¾   cup shredded mozzarella cheese
¾   cup grated Parmesan or Romano cheese
½   cup mayonnaise
1   (14-ounce) can artichoke hearts drained and chopped
1   (4-ounce) can chopped green chilies, drained

Preheat oven to 375 degrees.

Unroll crescent roll dough into 4 long rectangles and place crosswise on ungreased 15 x 10 x 1-inch baking pan, pressing over bottom and 1-inch up sides to form crust and seal gaps.

Bake about 10 minutes or until golden brown; remove from oven.

In a large bowl, mix cheeses, mayonnaise, artichokes and chilies and spread on top of crust. Return to oven and bake about 10-15 minutes or until topping is warm. Cut into 1-1½-inch squares and serve warm.

FUN FACT – The color of a chile is no indication of its spiciness, but size usually is – the smaller the pepper, the hotter it is.

Dill Weed Dip in a Bread Bowl

¾ cup mayonnaise
¾ cup sour cream
2 tablespoons dry minced onion
2 teaspoons "beau appetite" or
     "beau monde" seasoning
2 teaspoons dried dill weed
1 loaf round pumpernickel or rye
     bread

In a large bowl, mix mayonnaise, sour cream, onion, seasoning and dill weed. Refrigerate until chilled, at least 2 hours. Cut out center of pumpernickel or rye bread and tear into bite-size pieces. Spoon dip into the cut out bread crust. Place on a platter with cut out pieces arranged on platter around crust.

ACTIVITY – <u>Chautauqua/Lake Erie Wine Trail</u> – Glacial ridges have created a 20 mile stretch of land rich in loam on the shore of Lake Erie that provides optimal conditions for producing grapes. Vineyards in this area produce 60% of total grape tonnage in New York. This area also includes several wineries with free tours and tasting, farm markets and maple producers.

Salmon and Cheddar Ball

6	strips of bacon
14½	ounces canned or fresh cooked salmon
1	(8-ounce) package fat free cream cheese, room temperature
1	cup grated sharp Cheddar cheese
½	cup chopped Spanish (green) olives
3	tablespoons onion, minced
⅛	teaspoon hot pepper sauce (ex. Tabasco)
⅓	cup parsley, finely chopped
⅓	cup rosemary, finely chopped
½	cup parsley, finely chopped

In a skillet, cook bacon until crispy; drain grease, let cool and crumble. Flake* salmon. (If using canned salmon, drain first). In large mixing bowl, combine bacon, flaked salmon, cream cheese, Cheddar cheese, olives, onion, hot pepper sauce, parsley and rosemary; stir until thoroughly combined. Form mixture into a ball and refrigerate overnight.

After refrigerating, roll ball in ½ cup finely chopped parsley. Serve with mild crackers or toasts.

*To flake salmon use a fork to pull apart the fish by breaking off small pieces or layers.

FITNESS FACT – The average calories spent walking 2 miles per hour by a 150-pound person are 240 calories/hour. A lighter person burns fewer calories; a heavier person burns more.

Chicken Cheddar Quesadillas with Tomato and Corn Salsa

1½   cups purchased medium-hot chunky salsa verde

1   cup frozen corn kernels, thawed

1   cup chopped red onion, divided

¼   cup plus 6 tablespoons chopped fresh cilantro

      Salt and pepper to taste

1   pound chicken tenders (not breaded)

2   teaspoons chili powder

1   teaspoon ground cumin

4   tablespoons olive oil, divided

2   large garlic cloves, chopped

3   burrito-size flour tortillas (11-inches in diameter)

3   cups (packed) grated sharp Cheddar cheese (about 12-ounces)

In a small bowl blend salsa, corn, ¼ cup red onion, and ¼ cup cilantro. Season to taste with salt and pepper.

Sprinkle chicken with chili powder, cumin, salt, and pepper. Heat 2 tablespoons oil in heavy large skillet over medium-high heat. Add garlic and remaining ¾ cup onion and sauté 1 minute.

Add chicken and sauté until chicken is just cooked through, about 5 minutes.

Sprinkle half of 1 tortilla with ½ cup cheese. Place ⅓ chicken mixture atop cheese; sprinkle with 2 tablespoons cilantro and another ½ cup cheese. Fold tortilla in half. Repeat with remaining tortillas, cheese, chicken mixture, and cilantro.

Use one very large heavy skillet or 2 large ones. Heat 1 tablespoon oil in each of 2 heavy large skillets over medium-high heat or 2 tablespoons of oil in one skillet. Place quesadillas in hot skillet(s). Cook quesadillas until brown and cheese melts, about 4 minutes per side. Transfer quesadillas to work surface and cut into wedges. Arrange on platter; serve with salsa.

Yield: 6 appetizer servings

ACTIVITY – <u>Corn Maize, (Niagara and Orleans County)</u> – Day or night, these labyrinths of corn stalks are a challenge for all ages.

Italian Sausage Mushroom Caps

1	pound Italian sausage (Italian turkey sausage for a lower fat/lower calories)
24	fresh medium-sized mushrooms (1-1½-inch diameter) stems removed
1	(8-ounce) package cream cheese, room temperature
3	tablespoons minced fresh parsley
1	tablespoon minced fresh parsley
1	tablespoon grated Parmesan cheese

In a large skillet cook sausage over medium heat until no longer pink (for Italian turkey sausage until heated through), drain grease when done.

Wash mushroom caps and place on a microwave-safe plate. Microwave on high for 2 minutes and drain (time will vary, 2 minutes is for 1,100 watt microwave).

In a small mixing bowl combine sausage, cream cheese and 3 tablespoons parsley until well blended. Spoon equal amounts into mushroom caps on microwave-safe plate. Cover and microwave at 70% power until heated through, about 5-7 minutes and drain plate. Sprinkle with remaining parsley and Parmesan cheese.

Let stand for 5 minutes before serving.

TRIVIA – Buffalo was the first Metropolitan area to have electric street lights.

Wonton Wrapper Appetizers

1	(16-ounce) package wonton wrappers
1	pound sausage
1	cup shredded Monterey Jack cheese
1	cup shredded Cheddar cheese
½	cup chopped black olives
1	cup Ranch-style salad dressing

Preheat oven to 350 degrees.

Spray a miniature muffin pan with cooking spray. Insert wonton wrappers into the muffin pan to form small cups. Bake 5 minutes in the preheated oven. Allow the baked wrappers to cool. Remove form the pan.

In a medium bow, mix the sausage, Monterey Jack, Cheddar, black olives and Ranch-style dressing. Fill the baked wonton wrapper cups with the mixture.

Bake 10-15 minutes, until the sausage mixture is bubbly and slightly brown. Watch closely so the wonton wrappers do not burn.

Yield: 60 servings

ACTIVITY – Buffalo and Erie County Historical Society Museum (Erie) – an original building from the Pan American Exposition, offering the most comprehensive collection of Exposition artifacts in the permanent exhibit as well as a vast resource of genealogical information for Western New York.

Barley and Mushroom Soup

¼ ounce (about 3) dried mushrooms (porcini or shiitake)

1 cup hot water

1 tablespoon unsalted butter

1 tablespoon vegetable oil

5 ounces cleaned white mushrooms; remove stems and chop

1 small leek cleaned; dice the white part only

1 small onion, diced

1 medium celery stalk, diced

2 garlic cloves, minced

½ cup barley

4 cups beef broth or vegetable broth

1 tablespoon snipped dill

½ teaspoon salt

½ teaspoon pepper

Combine mushroom and hot water until mushrooms are soft. Remove the mushrooms and squeeze dry with paper towels. Reserve the soaking liquid. Dice the mushrooms finely and reserve. Heat butter and oil in a soup pot over medium-low heat until butter is melted. Add mushrooms, leek, onion, celery stalk, carrot, garlic and cook, stirring until tender but not browned.

Increase heat and add barley, cook until lightly toasted about 5 minutes. Stir in reserved diced mushrooms, strain the soaking liquid through a fine mesh sieve lined with a dampened paper towel and stir in the vegetable mixture and broth.

Bring to a boil, reduce heat and simmer, partially covered until barley is tender, about 40 minutes.

Season to taste with dill, salt and pepper. Serve immediately.

FUN FACT – Dill has a distinctive flavor in the delicate feathery leaves. Use on fish, salmon, in potato salad, egg dishes and cucumber salads.

Very Simple Pumpkin Soup

2	(15-ounce) cans pure pumpkin
4	cups water
1	cup half-and-half
1	garlic clove, pressed
¼	cup pure maple syrup
4	tablespoons unsalted butter
½	teaspoon Chinese five-spice powder*
	Salt and ground pepper to taste
4	ounces fresh shiitake mushrooms, stemmed, sliced

Bring first 4 ingredients to simmer in large saucepan over medium-high heat, whisking often. Whisk in syrup, 2 tablespoons butter, and five-spice powder. Simmer soup 10 minutes, whisking often. Season with salt and pepper to taste.

Soup can be made 1 day ahead. Chill until cold, then cover and keep chilled. Bring to simmer before serving.

Melt remaining 2 tablespoons butter in heavy medium skillet over medium-high heat. Add mushrooms; sauté until tender, about 10 minutes - divide soup among 6 bowls. Sprinkle soup with mushrooms; serve.

A blend of ground anise, cinnamon, star anise, cloves, and ginger available in the spice section of most supermarkets.

Yield: 6 servings

ACTIVITY – Harvest festivals and festivities flourish in October in all of the Western New York counties: apples, grapes, pumpkins and cider as well as music, arts and crafts abound.

Hearty Bean and Sausage Soup

4	ounces smoked sausage or chorizo, diced
1	cup chopped onion
1	clove garlic, minced
1	(16-ounce) can refried beans
1	(15-ounce) can Ranch-Style Texas beans, undrained
1	(14½-ounce) can chicken broth
1	(10-ounce) can diced tomatoes and green chilies, undrained
2	tablespoons lime juice
1	tablespoon chopped cilantro

In a 3-quart saucepan over medium heat, cook smoked sausage, stirring occasionally until lightly browned. Add onion and garlic; cook 5 minutes or until onion is tender. Add remaining ingredients; heat to boiling. Reduce heat; cover and simmer 15 minutes, stirring occasionally.

Yield: 6 servings

FUN FACT – Refried beans aren't really what they seem. Although their name seems like a reasonable translation of Spanish frijoles refritos, the fact is that these beans aren't fried twice. In Spanish, refritos literally means "well-fried," not "re-fried."

Corn and Pepper Chowder

1	large onion, chopped
1	medium sweet red pepper, chopped
1	teaspoon canola oil
3	tablespoons all-purpose flour
½	teaspoon ground cumin
2	cups water
1⅓	cups cubed potatoes
1	teaspoon chicken or vegetarian bouillon granules
¾	teaspoon salt
½	teaspoon white pepper
2	cups frozen corn
1	(12-ounce) can fat-free evaporated milk
¼	cup minced fresh cilantro or parsley

In a saucepan, sauté onion and red pepper in oil until tender. Sir in flour and cumin until blended. Gradually stir in water. Bring to a boil; cook and stir for 2 minutes or until thickened. Reduce heat; add the potatoes, bouillon, salt and pepper. Cover and cook for 10 minutes or until potatoes are tender. Add corn and milk. Cook, uncovered, 5 minutes longer or until heated through. Garnish with cilantro.

Yield: 6 servings

ACTIVITY – Curtain Up! Buffalo Theater District, Buffalo (Erie) – A date in September is the official opening night for the new season. Dinners, black tie events and celebration on Main Street following the first night's performances in the district.

Apple Stick Salad

½   cup white sugar

½   cup distilled white vinegar

3   tart apples, peeled, cored and julienned

⅔   cup chopped onion

½   cup chopped dill pickles

In a small bowl, combine sugar and vinegar.

In a medium bowl, mix together apples, onion and pickle. Toss with vinegar mixture. Refrigerate until thoroughly chilled.

Yield: 6 servings

FITNESS FACT – The average calories spent bicycling 6 miles per hour by a 150-pound person are 240 calories per hour. A lighter person burns fewer calories; a heavier person burns more.

Three Bean Salad

1	can green beans
1	can yellow wax beans
1	can red kidney beans
1	cup celery, chopped
1	green pepper, chopped
1	onion, chopped
¾	cup sugar

Dressing

1	teaspoon salt
½	teaspoon coarse black pepper
⅓	cup vegetable oil
⅔	cup vinegar

Mix the beans and chopped vegetables with sugar; refrigerate overnight. Mix dressing ingredients and combine with beans and vegetables.

Dressing can be varied by the type of vinegar that you use; herbed or wine vinegars are nice. You can also substitute garlic salt for plain salt or just add chopped garlic.

ACTIVITY – Devil's Hole State Park, Niagara Falls (Niagara) – Overlooks the whirlpool rapids with hiking trails to Niagara Fallsgorge, a popular location for fishermen. Picnic sites located at the bottom of the trail.

A Salad for Fall

1	head red leaf lettuce, torn
½	head romaine lettuce, torn
1	small red onion, sliced paper thin
1	ounce Gorgonzola or Roquefort cheese, crumbled
1	crisp Granny Smith Apple, cut into matchstick pieces
½	cup walnut pieces, toasted in the oven

Dressing

½	cup cider vinegar
2	tablespoons honey
⅓	cup raisins (dark or golden)
¼	cup toasted sesame seeds
½	teaspoon salt
¾	cup peanut oil
¼	cup toasted sesame oil

Arrange lettuce leaves on plates, top with red onion, cheese, apple, and walnut pieces just as they are removed from the oven, warm and toasted

Place all ingredients for dressing except the oils in a food processor and process until the raisins become a fine paste. While the machine is running, add both oils, one at a time, very slowly. Pour them in a stream no larger than a pencil lead.

Drizzle vinaigrette over salad and serve (or pass separately at table).

Yield: 1¼ cups

You will probably have a little dressing left over, but it keeps very well in the refrigerator. If it thickens when chilled, thin it a little with additional vinegar.

FUN FACTS – More apple varieties are grown in Central and Western New York than in any other part of the country.

Apple Salad

1   (8-ounce) can crushed pineapple
       with juice
½   cup sugar
1   tablespoon flour
1   egg
2   tablespoons apple cider vinegar
4   cups green apples cut into bite-
       size chunks
1½   cups crushed dry roasted peanuts
1   (8-ounce) container of whipped
       topping

Heat pineapple with juice, sugar, flour, egg and vinegar together in sauce pan until thick and bubbly, stirring constantly. Let cool.

Add cooled mixture to apples and nuts. Chill 1 hour in the refrigerator.

When chilled, mix in the whipped topping and serve.

ACTIVITY – <u>Dog Shows</u> – Spend a relaxing day at a dog show and see how your dog is supposed to act.

Macaroni and Tuna Salad

1	package macaroni
2	ribs diced celery
½	diced cucumber
½	cup finely diced onion
1	small can tuna, drained
¾	cup sweet pickle or relish
2	hard-boiled eggs
	Salt and pepper
1	teaspoon lemon juice
	Mayonnaise

Boil macaroni according to package directions, rinse and cool.

Chop celery, cucumber, and onion. Add tuna, pickle relish, and diced eggs. Mix all ingredients with macaroni. Add salt, pepper, and lemon juice to mayonnaise (use enough to your desired consistency). Mix well and chill.

FITNESS FACT – Riding uphill standing on your pedals burns about the same number of calories as sitting down.

Seven Layer Taco Salad

1   bag round tortilla chips
1   package taco seasoning
1   (8-ounce) container sour cream
1   cup grated Cheddar cheese
1   cup shredded lettuce
1   large tomato sliced in small
      pieces

Take the tortilla chips and make a base of chips on a large platter.

In a separate bowl, mix the taco seasoning and the sour cream together. Mold onto the taco shells in a sort of round shape.

Spread or sprinkle the cheese, lettuce, and tomato over the top with just a little more cheese. Spread some more chips around the sides.

Add a little salsa or guacamole to the dish.

ACTIVITY – Martin House Complex, Buffalo (Erie) – Tour one of the most historically significant Prairie style houses by America's most famous architect, Frank Lloyd Wright. The Darwin D. Martin House features seven types of art glass windows.

Country Raisin Rye Bread

2   cups whole wheat flour, divided
2   cups rye flour, divided
1   tablespoon active dry yeast
1   teaspoon salt
2   cups water
½   cup plus 1 teaspoon olive or
       canola oil, divided
½   cup molasses
½   cup honey
2¾ cups all-purpose flour
1   cup raisins

In a mixing bowl, combine 1 cup whole wheat flour, 1 cup rye flour, yeast and salt. In a saucepan, heat water, ½ cup oil, molasses and honey to 120-130 degrees. Add to dry ingredients; stir just until moistened. Stir in remaining whole wheat and rye flours and enough all-purpose flour to form a medium stiff dough.

Turn onto a floured surface; sprinkle with raisins. Knead until smooth and elastic, about 8-10 minutes. Grease a bowl with the remaining oil. Place dough in bowl, turning once to grease top. Cover and let rise in a warm place until doubled, about 1-1½ hours.

Punch dough down; turn onto a lightly floured surface. Divide into 4 pieces; shape each into a round loaf. Place 4-inches apart on 2 baking sheets coated with nonstick cooking spray. Cover and let rise until doubled, about 45 minutes. Bake at 325 degrees for 35-40 minutes or until golden brown.

Yield: 4 loaves (8 slices each)

FITNESS FACT – Strength training improves flexibility if you move your joints fully. Stretch after a muscle-building workout to help keep you limber.

Maple Oat Bread

1   cup old-fashioned oats
1   cup boiling water
1   (¼-ounce) package active dry
     yeast
⅓   cup warm water
     (110-115 degrees)
½   cup maple syrup
2   teaspoons canola oil
1½   teaspoons salt
3½-4 cups all-purpose flour

Topping
1   egg white, lightly beaten
2   tablespoons old-fashioned oats

In a blender or food processor, cover and process oats for 6-7 seconds or until coarsely chopped. Transfer to a small bowl; add boiling water. Let stand until mixture cools to 110-115 degrees. In a mixing bowl, dissolve yeast in ⅓ cup warm water; add syrup, oil, salt, oat mixture and 2 cups flour; beat until smooth. Stir in enough remaining flour to form a soft dough. Turn onto a lightly floured surface; knead until smooth and elastic, about 6-8 minutes. Place in a greased bowl, turning once to grease top. Cover and let rise in a warm place until doubled, about 1 hour.

Punch dough down. Turn onto a lightly floured surface. Shape into a flattened 9-inch round loaf. Place in a greased 9-inch round baking dish. Cover and let rise until doubled, about 45 minutes. Brush with egg white; sprinkle with oats. Bake at 325 degrees for 30-35 minutes or until golden brown. Remove from pan to a wire rack to cool.

Yield: 1 loaf (16 slices)

ACTIVITY – Flea Markets – this term most likely originates from Paris in the late 1800's, where Le Marche aux Puces (market of the fleas) was a popular outdoor shopping bazaar – suggesting that some of the goods or furnishings may have been infested...True or not, there is nothing better than a good deal! Find your good deal at Flea Markets around Western New York.

Banana-Walnut Muffins

1½	cups all-purpose flour
¾	cup sugar
¾	cup walnuts, coarsely chopped
1½	teaspoons baking soda
¼	teaspoon salt
½	cup walnut oil or canola oil
1	large egg
2-3	medium to large very ripe bananas, slightly mashed (Yield 1¼ cups)
3	tablespoons buttermilk

Preheat oven to 375 degrees.

Grease 10 standard muffin cups with butter or nonstick spray; fill unused cups ⅓ full with water to prevent warping. In bowl stir together flour, sugar, chopped walnuts, baking soda, and salt.

In another bowl whisk together oil, egg, mashed bananas, and buttermilk until blended. Add dry ingredients and beat well until evenly combined and creamy. Spoon batter into muffin cup filling it level with the rim of the cup.

Bake until golden, dry, and springy to the touch, 20-25 minutes. A toothpick inserted into the center of a muffin should come out clean. Transfer the pan to a wire rack and let cool for 5 minutes. Unmold muffins. Serve warm or room temperature.

Yield: 10 muffins

FUN FACTS – Bananas are actually herbs. Bananas die after fruiting, like all herbs do.

Currant Scones

3	cups all-purpose flour
3	tablespoons sugar
1	teaspoon baking soda
½	teaspoon salt
6	tablespoons (¾ stick) chilled unsalted butter, cut into pieces
⅓	cup dried currants
1	egg, beaten to blend
¾	cup plus 3 tablespoons buttermilk
1	tablespoon milk

Preheat over to 425 degrees.

Lightly flour large cookie sheet. Mix flour, sugar, baking soda and salt in large bowl. Add butter and rub in with fingertips until mixture resembles fine meal. Mix in currants. Mix in egg and enough buttermilk to form soft dough.

Turn dough out onto floured surface. Pat dough into ¾-inch thick round. Cut out rounds, using 2½-inch round cookie cutter. Gather scraps, press together and pat out to ¾-inch-thick round. Cut out additional rounds.

Transfer scones to prepared cookie sheet. Brush tops with milk. Bake until scones are golden brown and cooked through, about 18 minutes. Serve warm with butter or whipped cream and jam.

Yield: 15 servings

ACTIVITY – <u>Institute for Environmental Learning, Lyndonville (Orleans County)</u> – Observe and photograph common and endangered animals such as wolves, owls, eagles and cougars in their home at the Institute for Environmental Learning.

Chickpea-Stuffed Shells

18	uncooked jumbo pasta shells
1	(15-ounce) can chickpeas or garbanzo beans, rinsed and drained
2	egg whites
1	(15-ounce) carton reduced-fat ricotta cheese
½	cup minced fresh parsley
⅓	cup grated Parmesan cheese
1	small onion, quartered
1	garlic clove, minced
1	(28-ounce) jar meatless spaghetti sauce, divided
1½	cups (6-ounce) shredded mozzarella cheese

Cook pasta shells according to package directions. Meanwhile, place the chickpeas and egg whites in a food processor or blender; cover and process until smooth. Add the ricotta, parsley, Parmesan, onion and garlic; cover and process until well blended. Pour 1¼ cups of spaghetti sauce into an ungreased 13 x 9 x 2-inch baking dish; set aside.

Drain pasta shells; stuff with chickpea mixture. Place over sauce. Drizzle with remaining sauce. Bake, uncovered, at 350 degrees for 30 minutes. Sprinkle with mozzarella cheese. Bake 5-10 minutes longer or until cheese is melted and sauce is bubbly.

Yield: 6 servings

One serving (3 stuffed shells) equals 508 calories, 19 grams fat (9 grams saturated fat), 42 milligrams cholesterol, 1066 milligrams sodium, 58 grams carbohydrate, 8 grams fiber, 27 grams protein.

FITNESS FACT – Adding 10 pounds of muscle to our bodies can translate into burning an additional 350-500 calories each day!

Baked Stuffed Zucchini

1   medium zucchini
6   large fresh mushrooms, finely
        chopped
1   green onion, finely chopped
1   tablespoon butter or stick
        margarine
½   cup white wine or chicken broth
⅛   teaspoon salt
     Dash white pepper
2   teaspoons grated Parmesan
        cheese

Cut zucchini in half lengthwise. Scoop out pulp, leaving a ¼-inch shell. Chop pulp; set shells aside. In nonstick skillet, sauté the zucchini pulp, mushrooms and onion in butter for 3-4 minutes or until tender. Add wine or broth. Reduce heat; simmer, uncovered, 10-12 minutes or until liquid has evaporated. Stir in salt and pepper.

Place zucchini shells in saucepan and cover with water; bring to a boil. Cook for 2 minutes; drain. Fill shells with mushroom mixture. Sprinkle with cheese. Broil 3-4 inches from the heat for 3-4 minutes or until lightly browned.

Yield: 2 servings

ACTIVITY – Iroquois Wildlife Refuge, Basom (Orleans) – Wooded swamps, marshlands, wet meadows, pasture and cropland are all part of this 11,000 acre of wildlife refuge. Attend the annual hatching of the endangered bald eagles.

Creole Catfish Fillets

Yogurt Sauce

3   tablespoons reduced-fat plain yogurt
2   tablespoons finely chopped onion
1   tablespoon fat-free mayonnaise
1   tablespoon Dijon mustard
1   tablespoon ketchup
½   teaspoon dried thyme
¼   teaspoon grated lemon peel

Catfish Fillets

1   teaspoon paprika
½   teaspoon onion powder
¼   teaspoon salt
⅛   teaspoon cayenne pepper
4   catfish fillets (4-ounces each)
4   lemon wedges

For yogurt sauce: in a bowl, combine the first seven ingredients. Cover and refrigerate until serving.

For Catfish fillets: in another bowl, combine paprika, onion powder, salt and cayenne; rub over both sides of fillets. Grill, covered, in a grill basket coated with nonstick cooking spray over medium-hot heat, or broil 6-inches from the heat for 5-6 minutes on each side or until fish flakes easily with a fork.

Serve with lemon wedges and yogurt sauce.

Yield: 4 servings

One serving (1 fillet with about 1 tablespoon sauce) equals 182 calories, 9 grams fat (2 grams saturated fat), 54 milligrams cholesterol, 382 milligrams sodium, 5 grams carbohydrate, 1 gram fiber, 19 gram protein. Diabetic Exchanges: 3 lean meat, ½ fat.

FITNESS FACT – Evidence suggests that even moderate-intensity activities can have both short-and long-term benefits. If done daily, they help lower your risk of heart disease. Such activities include walking, stair climbing, gardening, yard work, moderate to heavy housework, dancing and home exercise.

Lemon Pan Seared Black Sea Bass

10 Black Sea Bass filets, (5-6 ounces each)
½ cup extra-virgin olive oil
Coarse salt
Ground pepper
2 tablespoons lemon juice
1 cup flour
½ bunch oregano, stems removed and rough chopped

Preheat oven to 350 degrees.

Using pastry brush, coat fish with olive oil. Season fish with salt, pepper, and lemon juice. Lightly dredge filets in flour. Shake off excess flour. In a preheated skillet (one that can be used in the oven), sear fish skin side down, until lightly browned. Using spatula, turn fish and finish in the skillet in oven.

Cook about 4 minutes or until firm to the touch. Place on heated serving dish and garnish with chopped oregano.

ACTIVITY – Erie Canal Culvert Tunnel near Medina (Orleans) – is the only tunnel which passes under the 350 long Erie Canal.

Vegetable Pork Sauté

5	tablespoons all-purpose flour, divided
1	teaspoon Italian seasoning
½	teaspoon salt
¼	teaspoon pepper
1	pound boneless pork, cubed
5	tablespoons butter, divided
1	tablespoon olive oil
1	medium onion, halved and sliced
2	celery ribs, sliced
½	cup sliced fresh mushrooms
1	medium zucchini, halved and sliced
1	medium tomato, diced
1½	cups chicken broth
1	tablespoon balsamic vinegar
	Hot cooked rice

In a large re-sealable plastic bag, combine 3 tablespoons flour, Italian seasoning, salt and pepper. Add pork; seal bag and shake to coat. In a large skillet over medium-high heat, brown pork in 3 tablespoons butter and oil; remove and keep warm.

In the same skillet, sauté the onion, celery and mushrooms in remaining butter for 5 minutes. Add pork and zucchini; sauté until meat juices run clear and vegetables are tender.

Stir in tomato. Place remaining flour in a small bowl; stir in broth and vinegar until smooth. Add to skillet. Bring to boil; cook and stir for 2 minutes or until thickened. Serve with rice.

Yield: 4 servings

FUN FACT – Half of the world's population live on a staple diet of rice.

Stuffed Chicken Breasts

4   boneless skinless chicken breast
    halves (6-ounces each)
    Salt and pepper to taste
1   (6-ounce) package chicken
    stuffing mix
½   cup chopped pecans
2   tablespoons butter
1   (10¾-ounce) can condensed
    cream of mushroom soup,
    undiluted

Preheat oven to 400 degrees.

Flatten chicken to ¼-inch thickness; sprinkle with salt and pepper. Prepare stuffing mix according to package directions. Meanwhile, in a small skillet, sauté the pecans in butter until lightly browned; add to stuffing.

Place ½ cup stuffing down the center of each chicken breast half; roll up and secure with a toothpick. Place seam side down in a greased shallow 1-quart baking dish.

Spoon soup over chicken; sprinkle with remaining stuffing. Cover and bake at 400 degrees for 25-30 minutes or until chicken juices run clear. Remove toothpicks before serving.

Yield: 4 servings

ACTIVITY – YMCA Turkey Trot, Buffalo (Erie) – an annual 8K (4.97 miles) run held on Thanksgiving. Proceeds raised from race help provide scholarship assistance to needy families who participate in YMCA programs such as childcare and other youth developing programs.

Beef Burgundy over Noodles

½   pound boneless beef sirloin steak, cut into ¼-inch strips
2   tablespoons diced onion
2   teaspoons butter
1½   cups quartered fresh mushrooms
¾   cup red wine or beef broth
¼   cup plus 2 tablespoons water, divided
3   tablespoons minced fresh parsley, divided
1   bay leaf
1   whole clove
¼   teaspoon salt
⅛   teaspoon pepper
1   tablespoon all-purpose flour
½   teaspoon browning sauce, optional
1½   cups hot cooked egg noodles

In a Dutch oven or nonstick skillet, brown beef and onion in butter over medium heat. Add the mushrooms, wine or broth, ¼ cup water, 2 tablespoons parsley, bay leaf, clove, salt and pepper. Bring to a boil. Reduce heat; cover and simmer for 1 hour or until beef is tender.

Combine flour and remaining water until smooth; stir into beef mixture. Bring to boil; cook and stir 2 minutes or until thickened. Discard bay leaf and clove. Stir in browning sauce if desired. Serve over noodles. Sprinkle with remaining parsley.

Yield: 2 servings

One serving equals 410 calories, 12 grams fat (5 grams saturated fat), 125 milligrams cholesterol, 403 milligrams sodium, 37 grams carbohydrate, 2 grams fiber, and 33 grams protein. Diabetic Exchanges: 3 lean meat, 2 starch, 1 vegetable, ½ fat.

FUN FACT – According to a Kraft Cheese Family Study, America's top family main dishes are spaghetti, 52%, grilled chicken, 50%, and Pizza, 49%. Favorite side dishes are baked potato, salad and pasta.

Penne Sausage Casserole

1	(1-pound) package penne or medium tube pasta
1	medium-sized green pepper, chopped
1	small onion, chopped
1	tablespoon olive or canola oil
1	pound turkey Italian sausage links, casings removed
3	cups fat-free meatless spaghetti sauce
1½	cups (6-ounce) shredded part-skim mozzarella cheese
¼	cup grated Parmesan cheese

Cook pasta according to package directions; drain. In a large skillet, sauté green pepper and onion in oil for 6-7 minutes. Add sausage; cook and stir until sausage is no longer pink. Drain. Stir in spaghetti sauce and pasta.

Transfer to a 3-quart baking dish coated with nonstick cooking spray. Cover and bake at 350 degrees for 15-20 minutes. Uncover; sprinkle with cheeses. Bake 5-10 minutes longer or until cheese is melted.

Yield: 9 servings

One serving (1 cup) equals 276 calories, 11 grams fat (4 grams saturated fat), 40 milligrams cholesterol, 948 milligrams sodium, 25 grams carbohydrate, 1 gram fiber, 18 grams protein. Diabetic Exchanges: 2 lean meat, 1½ starch, 1 fat.

ACTIVITY – Ballroom Dancing – with or without a partner, discover ballroom dancing in your community through an association, adult community education, community center or professional instruction.

Dilled Pot Roast

2	teaspoons dill, divided
1	teaspoon salt
¼	teaspoon pepper
1	boneless chuck roast (2½ pounds)
¼	cup water
1	tablespoon cider vinegar
3	tablespoons all-purpose flour
¼	cup cold water
1	(8-ounce) cup sour cream
½	teaspoon browning sauce, optional
	Hot cooked rice

In a small bowl, combine 1 teaspoon dill, salt and pepper. Sprinkle over both sides of roast. Place in a 3-quart slow cooker. Add water and vinegar. Cover and cook on low for 7-8 hours or until the meat is tender.

Remove meat and keep warm. In a small bowl, combine flour and remaining dill; stir in cold water until smooth. Gradually stir into slow cooker. Cover and cook on high for 30 minutes or until thickened. Stir in sour cream and browning sauce if desired; heat through. Slice meat. Serve with sour cream sauce and rice.

Yield: 6-8 servings

FUN FACT – Riviana reports that it takes 300 gallons of water to grow one pound of rice.

Sweet-and-Sour Meatballs over Rice

1	(20-ounce) can unsweetened pineapple chunks
1	egg
1	cup soft bread crumbs
1	garlic clove, minced
1	teaspoon salt
¼	teaspoon pepper
1½	pounds lean ground beef
2	teaspoons canola oil
2	large green peppers
1	cup chicken broth
½	cup sugar
3	tablespoons cornstarch
½	cup cider vinegar
3	tablespoons reduced-sodium soy sauce
6	cups hot cooked rice

Drain pineapple, reserving ½ cup juice (discards remaining juice or saves for another use). Set juice and pineapple aside. In a bowl, combine the egg with next 4 ingredients. Crumble beef over mixture and mix well. Shape into 40 meatballs.

In a nonstick skillet, brown meatballs in oil; drain. Cut green peppers into chunks. Add broth, peppers and reserved pineapple to meatballs. Bring to boil. Reduce heat; simmer, uncovered, for 5-7 minutes.

Meanwhile, combine sugar and cornstarch in a bowl. Stir in vinegar, soy sauce and reserved pineapple mixture. Bring to boil; cook and stir for 2 minutes or until thickened. Serve over rice.

Yield: 8 servings

One serving (¾ cup meatball mixture with ¾ cup rice) equals 456 calories, 10 gram fat (3 grams saturated fat), 58 milligrams cholesterol, 755 milligrams sodium, 66 grams carbohydrate, 2 grams fiber, 23 grams protein. Diabetic Exchanges: 3 lean meat, 2½ starches, 1½ vegetable, and 1 fat.

ACTIVITY – <u>Bowling</u> – Evidence of bowling may have dated as early as 3200 BC in Egypt. The first written account in American Literature was by Washington Irving when Rip Van Winkle awakens to the "sound of crashing nine pins". Bowling Alleys are located throughout Western New York.

Garlic Potato Wedges

4	pounds small red potatoes, cut into wedges
1/3	cup olive or canola oil, divided
16	unpeeled garlic cloves
2	tablespoons minced fresh rosemary or 2 tablespoons dried rosemary, crushed
1	teaspoon salt
1/3	cup white wine vinegar or cider vinegar
4	teaspoons Dijon mustard
3	teaspoons sugar
1/4	teaspoon pepper
1/3	cup chopped green onions

In a large bowl, combine potatoes, 1 tablespoon of oil, garlic, rosemary and salt. Pour into two 15 x 10 x 1-inch baking pans coated with nonstick cooking spray. Bake, uncovered, at 450 degrees for 25-30 minutes or until potatoes are tender, stirring every 10 minutes.

In a small bowl, combine vinegar, mustard, sugar, pepper and remaining oil until smooth. Squeeze roasted garlic into vinegar mixture (discard skins). Pour over potatoes and toss to coat. Sprinkle with onions.

Yield: 8 servings

FUN FACT – There are certain fruits and vegetables that should not be stored together. Apples give off a gas called ethylene, which will turn carrots bitter. Potatoes will spoil faster when stored with onions.

Low-Fat Cheesy Scalloped Potatoes

5	large potatoes, peeled and thinly sliced
3	tablespoons all-purpose flour
1½	teaspoons salt
¼	teaspoon pepper
1¼	cups shredded reduced-fat Cheddar cheese, divided
3	ounces reduced-fat Swiss cheese slices, finely chopped (¾ cup), divided
2	medium onions, finely chopped
1½	cups 2% milk
2	tablespoons minced fresh parsley

Place ⅓ of the potatoes in a shallow 3-quart baking dish coated with nonstick cooking spray. In a small bowl, combine the flour, salt and pepper; sprinkle ½ over potatoes. Sprinkle with ¼ cup of each cheese and half the onions. Repeat layers. Top with remaining potatoes. Pour milk over all.

Cover and bake at 350 degrees for 50-60 minutes or until potatoes are nearly tender. Sprinkle with remaining cheeses. Bake, uncovered, 10 minutes longer or until cheese is melted and potatoes are tender. Sprinkle with parsley.

Yield: 8 servings

ACTIVITY – Pumpkin Picking (Chautauqua) – Pick your-own-farms are easy to find in Chautauqua County and the most active picking time would be between October 1st and 15th.

Italian Rice

2   garlic cloves, minced
2   teaspoons olive or canola oil
8   cups fresh spinach (about
     10-ounces), chopped
1   tablespoon balsamic vinegar
½   teaspoon salt
⅛   teaspoon pepper
2   cups hot cooked rice
½   cup chopped roasted sweet red
     peppers

In a large nonstick skillet, sauté garlic in oil 1 minute. Stir in spinach. Cover and cook 3-4 minutes or until tender; drain well. Add vinegar, salt and pepper. Stir in rice and sweet red peppers until combined. Cook and stir until heated through.

Yield: 4 servings

FUN FACT – Sage is assertive, with a hint of lemon. Use with pork, in poultry stuffing and bean dishes. Sprinkle chopped leaves over vegetables such as squash and eggplant.

Sweet and Savory Apple Stuffing

1	medium tart apple, peeled and chopped
2	celery ribs, chopped
1	medium onion, chopped
¼	cup minced fresh parsley
3	green onions, thinly sliced
2	tablespoons chopped celery leaves
2	tablespoons butter or stick margarine
½	cup tropical medley dried fruit mix
¼	cup dried cranberries
¼	cup chopped pecans
1	teaspoon poultry seasoning
½	teaspoon salt
½	teaspoon rubbed sage
¼	teaspoon pepper
1	(14½-ounce) can reduced-sodium chicken broth
1½	cups water
1	(12-ounce) unseasoned stuffing croutons

In a skillet, cook apple, celery, onion, parsley, green onions and celery leaves in butter until tender. Stir in fruit mix, cranberries, pecans, poultry seasoning, salt, sage and pepper; mix well. Stir in broth, water and stuffing. Toss to coat evenly.

Transfer to a 13 x 9 x 2-inch baking dish coated with nonstick cooking spray. Cover and bake at 350 degrees for 20 minutes. Uncover; bake 10-15 minutes longer or until heated through and lightly browned.

Yield: 12 servings

ACTIVITY – A hikers' paradise for the well-seasoned trekker and the casual walker. Letchworth State Park has 14,350 acres, 67.2 miles of trails, and the Genesee Gorge, New York's "Grand Canyon".

Twice-Baked Acorn Squash

2	medium acorn squash (about 1 ½ pounds each)
1	(10-ounce) package frozen chopped spinach, thawed and squeezed dry
2	bacon strips, cooked and crumbled
10	tablespoons shredded Parmesan cheese, divided
2	tablespoons thinly sliced green onion
1	tablespoon butter or stick margarine, softened
¼	teaspoon salt
⅛	teaspoon cayenne pepper

Cut squash in half; discard seeds. Place squash upside down on a cookie sheet coated with nonstick cooking spray. Bake at 350 degrees for 50-55 minutes or until tender. Scoop out squash leaving a ¼-inch shell.

In a bowl, combine squash pulp, spinach, bacon, 6 tablespoons Parmesan cheese, green onion, butter, salt and cayenne; spoon into shells. Sprinkle with remaining Parmesan cheese. Bake 25-30 minutes or until heated through and top is golden brown.

Yield: 4 servings

Scalloped Squash and Apples

2	pounds butternut squash, peeled, seeded and cut into 1-inch pieces
2	large apples, peeled and cut into 1-inch pieces
¼	cup packed brown sugar
2	tablespoons corn syrup
2	tablespoons orange juice
1	tablespoon butter or stick margarine, melted
2	teaspoons grated orange peel
½	teaspoon salt

Layer squash and apples in an 11 x 7 x 2-inch baking dish coated with nonstick cooking spray. In a bowl, combine the remaining ingredients. Pour over squash and apples. Cover and bake at 350 degrees for 35-40 minutes or until tender.

Yield: 6 servings

ACTIVITY – <u>Roycroft Inn</u> originally opened in 1905 to serve the thousands who came to the Roycroft Arts and Crafts Community. Although the restaurant has been open for many years, the rooms were closed around 1940, only to reopen in 1995.

Pumpkin Pie

Pastry for 9-inch pie
2   cups cooked puréed pumpkin
1   cup brown sugar
5   eggs, lightly beaten
2   cups heavy cream
½   teaspoon salt
1   teaspoon cinnamon
¼   teaspoon ground cloves
½   teaspoon mace
⅓   cup cognac or 3 tablespoons
    maple sugar
4   tablespoons finely chopped
    crystallized ginger

Line a 9-inch pie tin with pastry and place foil on top. Fill with dry beans or ceramic pie weights (to keep unfilled pie crust from shrinking during baking) and bake in a 400 degree oven for 10 minutes. Remove the beans and weights.

Combine the pumpkin with the sugar, eggs, cream, seasonings and cognac and blend well. Pour through a strainer into the pie shell. Sprinkle with chopped crystallized ginger and bake in a 375 degree oven for 30-35 minutes, or until the pumpkin is set. Serve slightly warm with cheese or whipped cream, or both.

ACTIVITY – The Chautauqua Institution is listed on the National Register of Historic Places. It was founded in 1874.

Apple Pie

Pastry

¾   cup cake flour
1¾   cups all-purpose flour
     Scant teaspoon salt
1   tablespoon sugar
     Large pinch Rumford Baking
       Powder
1   tablespoon buttermilk powder
4   tablespoons Crisco shortening
1   tablespoon lard
1   tablespoon lemon juice or white
       vinegar ADDED TO:
5-7 tablespoons ice water
1   stick plus ⅓ stick butter, frozen in
       advance

Filling

10   apples, peeled and sliced thinly
¼   teaspoon nutmeg
½   teaspoon ginger
¼   teaspoon cinnamon
½   cup white sugar
     Sprinkle of vanilla
2   tablespoons butter
2   tablespoons flour, cornstarch, or
       arrowroot for thickening
2   tablespoons brown sugar
     Lemon juice
     Sprinkle of mace (optional)

Combine dry ingredients. Mix together Crisco and lard in metal bowl. Sprinkle with flour mixture. Chill in refrigerator for 15 minutes. Remove butter from freezer and slice into ½-inch chunks. Add to bowl. Work butter and shortenings together into flour with fingers or a pastry blender, leaving large chunks, the size of walnuts. The purpose is to coat the butter particles with flour, but not to allow the butter or shortenings to melt. Do not overwork the mixture.

Add the lemon juice or vinegar to ice water and stir quickly into dry ingredients. Mix briefly, less than 45 seconds; leave large unincorporated pockets of butter and shortening. If mixture is beginning to melt, refrigerate briefly.

Gather mixture together into a flat disc, approximately 1-inch thick, wrap in plastic wrap and refrigerate for at least ½ hour or up to 2 days. Freeze to reserve longer than 2 days. The ½ hour rest is necessary so that the dough will become easier to roll out. The buttermilk powder and/or lemon juice also helps relax dough and prevent gluten, which can make for a tough crust.

For filling, the best combination of apples consists of mostly Granny Smith apples and a few Cortland types. Granny Smith apples retain their shape when cooked and provide tartness and flavor; Cortland apples cook down into applesauce.

Mix nutmeg, ginger, and cinnamon with sugar. Sprinkle sugar with a few drops of pure vanilla extract. Work butter and 2 tablespoons flour or other thickener into the sugar. Slice apples into thin wedges and place apples into pre-rolled out and fitted pie crust, packing apples in tightly, since they will cook down significantly. Mound apples higher in center. Sprinkle over apples juice of ½ lemon, then sprinkle sugar-spice mixture evenly over apples. Roll out and place top crust, fluting edges to seal tightly and create several vent holes to allow steam to escape.

Brush top of crust with a mixture of 1 egg white and 1 tablespoon of water or with a little cream. Sprinkle with 1 teaspoon sugar.

One method of making a nice base for your apple pie is to peel a portion of the apples, placing the skins, cores, lemon peels, cinnamon sticks, and fresh grated ginger, into a saucepan with sugar and ½ cup of water or apple juice. Simmer over low heat for about 1 hour and strain, reserving the liquid. Thicken ½ cup of the strained liquid with 1-2 teaspoons of cornstarch or arrowroot and cool. Add ¼ teaspoon vanilla, the sliced and peeled apples, and pour into the pie shell. This is a nice variation when you don't have Cortland apples to mix in with the granny smiths because it keeps the pie from being too dry. The liquid is enough for one 10-inch pie about 4-inches tall at center. Adjust according to your pie size.

For flakier pie crust, reserve ⅓ stick of butter and slice lengthwise, ⅛-inch thick. Place strips of butter onto dough and fold into thirds before refrigerating for ½ hour resting period.

FUN FACT – The best way to store apples at home is in a plastic bag (to help retain moisture) in the refrigerator. That way, they stay crisp longer.

Dark Chocolate Cupcakes with Peanut Butter Filling

¾ cup plus 2 tablespoons cocoa powder (not Dutch process)
½ cup boiling water
1 cup buttermilk
1¾ cups all-purpose flour
1¼ teaspoons baking soda
¼ teaspoon baking powder
¼ teaspoon salt
1½ sticks plus 3 tablespoons unsalted butter, softened
1½ cups granulated sugar
2 large eggs, at room temperature
1 teaspoon pure vanilla extract
1 cup creamy peanut butter
⅔ cup confectioners' sugar
1 cup heavy cream
8 ounces semi-sweet chocolate, chopped

Preheat the oven to 350 degrees and position 2 racks in the lower and middle third of the oven.

Line 24 muffin cups with paper or foil liners. Put the cocoa powder in a medium heatproof bowl. Add the boiling water and whisk until a smooth paste forms. Whisk in the buttermilk until combined. In a medium bowl, sift the flour with the baking soda, baking powder and salt. In a large bowl, using an electric mixer, beat 1½ sticks of the butter with the granulated sugar until light and fluffy, about 3 minutes. Beat in the eggs and vanilla, and then beat in the dry ingredients in 2 batches, alternating with the cocoa mixture. Carefully spoon the cupcake batter into the lined muffin cups, filling them about ⅔ full. Bake for 20-22 minutes, or until the cupcakes are springy. Let the cupcakes cool in the pans for 5 minutes, and then transfer them to wire racks to cool completely.

In a medium bowl, beat the peanut butter with the remaining 3 tablespoons of butter until creamy. Sift the confectioners' sugar into the bowl and beat until light and fluffy, about 2 minutes. Spoon all but 3 tablespoons of the peanut butter filling into a pastry bag fitted with a ¼-inch star tip. Holding a cupcake in your hand, plunge the tip into the top of the cake, pushing it about ¾-inch deep. Gently squeeze the pastry bag to fill the cupcake, withdrawing it slowly as you squeeze; you will feel the cupcake expand slightly as you fill it. Scrape any filling from the top of the cupcake and repeat until all of the cupcakes are filled.

In a small saucepan, bring the heavy cream to a simmer. Off the heat, add the semi-sweet chocolate to the cream and let stand for 5 minutes, and then whisk the melted chocolate into the cream until smooth. Let the chocolate icing stand until slightly cooled and thickened, about 15 minutes. Dip the tops of the cupcakes into the icing, letting the excess drip back into the pan. Transfer the cupcakes to racks and let stand for 5 minutes. Dip the tops of the cupcakes again and transfer them to racks. Spoon the remaining 3 tablespoons of peanut butter filling into the pastry bag and pipe tiny rosettes on the tops of the cupcakes.

The cupcakes are best served the same day they are made, but they can be refrigerated overnight in an airtight container.

Yield: 24 cupcakes

ACTIVITY – Murphy Orchards, Burt (Niagara) – offers a variety of agricultural, environmental and Underground Railroad Heritage guided group tours by reservation. A working farm for over 150 years with a unique view of American history.

Guinness Ginger Cake

1	cup Guinness stout
1	cup molasses
½	tablespoon baking soda
3	large eggs
½	cup granulated sugar
½	cup firmly packed dark brown sugar
¾	cup grape seed or vegetable oil
2	cups all-purpose flour
2	tablespoons ground ginger
1½	teaspoons baking powder
¾	teaspoon ground cinnamon
¼	teaspoon ground cloves
¼	teaspoon freshly grated nutmeg
⅛	teaspoon ground cardamom
1	tablespoon grated, peeled fresh gingerroot

Preheat oven to 350 degrees.

Butter a 9 x 5-inch loaf pan, line the bottom and sides with parchment, and grease the parchment. Alternatively, butter and flour a 6-cup Bundt pan.

In a large saucepan over high heat, combine the stout and molasses and bring to a boil. Turn off the heat and add the baking soda. Allow to sit until the foam dissipates.

Meanwhile, in a bowl, whisk together the eggs and both sugars. Whisk in the oil.

In a separate bowl, whisk together the flour, ground ginger, baking powder, cinnamon, cloves, nutmeg, and cardamom.

Combine the stout mixture with the egg mixture, then whisk this liquid into the flour mixture, half at a time. Add the fresh ginger and stir to combine.

Pour the batter into the loaf pan and bake for 1 hour, or until the top springs back when gently pressed. Do not open the oven until the gingerbread is almost done, or the center may fall slightly. Transfer to a wire rack to cool.

FUN FACT – The ice cream soda was invented in 1874 by Robert Green. He was serving a mixture of syrup, sweet cream and carbonated water at a celebration in Philadelphia. He ran out of cream and substituted ice cream.

Carrot Cake

2	cups all-purpose flour
2	teaspoons baking soda
1	teaspoon salt
1	teaspoon ground cinnamon
2	cups sugar
1¼	cups canola oil
4	large eggs
3	cups grated peeled carrots
1¼	cups coarsely chopped walnuts
2	tablespoons minced peeled ginger

Icing

10	ounces cream cheese, room temperature
5	tablespoons unsalted butter, room temperature
2½	cups powdered sugar
¼	cup pure maple syrup
12	walnut halves (for garnish)

For cake: Preheat oven to 350 degrees.

Butter two 9-inch-diameter cake pans. Line bottom of pans with waxed paper. Butter and flour paper; tap out excess flour. Whisk flour, baking soda, salt and cinnamon in medium bowl to blend. Whisk sugar and oil in large bowl until well blended. Whisk in eggs 1 at a time. Add flour mixture and stir until blended. Stir in carrots, walnuts and ginger. Divide batter between prepared pans.

Bake cakes until tester inserted into center comes out clean, about 40 minutes. Cool cakes in pans 15 minutes. Turn out onto racks. Peel off waxed paper; cool cakes completely.

For icing: Using electric mixer beat cream cheese and butter in large bowl until light and fluffy. Add powdered sugar and beat at low speed until well blended. Beat in maple syrup. Chill until just firm enough to spread, 30 minutes.

Place 1 cake layer on platter. Spread with ¾ cup icing. Top with second layer. Spread remaining icing over entire cake. Arrange walnut halves around top edge. (Can be made 1 day ahead. Cover with cake dome; chill. Let stand at room temperature 30 minutes before serving.)

Yield: 12 servings

ACTIVITY – Busti Apple Festival (Chautauqua) – This event is held every year for people to come and enjoy delicious apples and refreshing apple cider while learning and watching how it is made at the cider mill.

Cookie Cannoli with Coffee Cream

4	tablespoons unsalted butter, at room temperature
⅔	cup sugar
2	large egg whites, at room temperature
½	cup all-purpose flour
½	teaspoon finely grated orange zest
¾	teaspoon pure vanilla extract
	Pinch of salt
1	cup mascarpone
1	cup heavy cream
1	teaspoon pure coffee extract
	Confectioners' sugar, for dusting

Preheat oven to 375 degrees.

Line 2 baking sheets with parchment paper. Trace three 4-inch circles on each with a pencil; turn the parchment over.

In a medium bowl, using an electric mixer beat the butter with ⅓ cup of the sugar until fluffy. Add the egg whites and beat until blended. Add the flour, orange zest, ¼ teaspoon of the vanilla and the salt and beat until smooth.

Using a small offset spatula, evenly spread 1 tablespoon of the batter into each circle. Bake the cookies, 1 sheet at a time, for 8-9 minutes, or until lightly golden and browned around the edges. Immediately roll each cookie around a 1-inch wide tube or dowel and let cool until crisp. Carefully remove the Cannoli from the tubes and transfer to a wire rack. Repeat twice with the remaining batter to make 18 cookies.

In a medium bowl, using an electric mixer beat the mascarpone at medium speed with the cream, the coffee extract and the remaining ⅓ cup sugar and ½ teaspoon of vanilla until firm peaks form.

Fill a pastry bag fitted with a ½-inch star tip with the coffee cream. Carefully pipe the mascarpone cream into both ends of the cookies, finishing with a small rosette at each end. Transfer the Cannoli to a platter, dust them with confectioners' sugar and serve.

The cookies can be stored in an airtight container at room temperature for up to 3 days.

FUN FACT – There are over 400 varieties of natural cheeses!

Grape Pastries with Cream

Pastry Cream

3   large egg yolks

⅓   cup sugar, depending on sweetness of grapes (Taste. No sugar may be needed.)

2½   tablespoons all-purpose flour

     Pinch of salt

1   cup whole milk

1   teaspoon vanilla

1½   tablespoons unsalted butter

     Wax paper

     Extra butter

Pastry

1   sheet frozen puff pastry (½ pound), thawed

     Flour

2   teaspoons sugar

4   cups red and green grapes

2   tablespoons red currant jelly

For Pastry cream: In a large bowl, whisk together yolks and ½ of sugar, then whisk in flour and a pinch salt. Stir together milk and remaining sugar in a heavy saucepan and bring just to a boil over moderate heat. Whisk ½ of hot milk and sugar mixture into yolks, pour into remaining milk and sugar mixture in heavy sauce pan. Bring to a boil over moderate heat, whisking constantly, until very thick. Remove from heat and stir in vanilla and butter until incorporated or thoroughly combined. Chill in a bowl and cover with a buttered piece of wax paper until cold, about 1 hour.

For Pastry: Preheat oven to 425 degrees while pastry cream chills. Open puff pastry sheet on a lightly floured surface and roll out to a 14 x 12-inch rectangle. Cut pastry sheet to form 4 rectangles; brush ⅓-inch of edges lightly with water and fold in the wet edges. Brush off excess flour and the folded edge with back of a fork to seal. Brush edges lightly with water again and sprinkle with sugar. Prick insides of shells all over with fork to prevent cracking while baking. Bake on a large baking sheet at 425 degrees in middle of oven until crust is golden brown, about 10-15 minutes. Transfer to a rack and gently flatten puff pastry inside sealed to deflate; cool completely.

Halve grapes and seed if necessary; place in a medium bowl. Melt jelly in a sauce pan or microwave, stir; pour into bowl with grapes and toss. Spread pastry cream in shells with a spatula and top with grape and jelly mixture. Serve immediately.

Yield: 4 servings

ACTIVITY – The 1820's <u>Darwin R. Barker House in Fredonia</u> is now a museum featuring local history.

Strawberry Crisps

Cooking spray
4   cups strawberries cut into quarters
1   tablespoon light brown sugar
3   tablespoons light brown sugar
¼   cup regular oats
3   tablespoons all-purpose flour
3   tablespoons melted butter
2   tablespoons toasted, chopped
    almonds

Preheat oven to 300 degrees. Coat four 8-ounce ramekins with cooking spray.

Toss strawberries with 1 tablespoon light brown sugar. Spoon 1 cup of strawberries in each ramekin.

Combine all remaining ingredients, stir until crumbly. Sprinkle an even amount of crumbly mixture over each ramekin filled with strawberries.

Place ramekins on baking sheet and bake for 20 minutes.

229 calories (44% from fat), fat 12 grams (6g sat, 4g mono, 1g poly), 4 grams protein, 30 grams carbohydrate, 4 grams fiber

FUN FACT – Strawberries are the 3rd most valuable fruit crop grown in New York and New York is 7th nationally in strawberry production.

Poached Pears

4	Bosc pears
1	cup water
1	cup dry white wine
2	tablespoons sugar
2	tablespoons honey
4	dried apricots
2	(3 x ½-inch) lemon rind strips
1	(3-inch) piece vanilla bean, split lengthwise
1	whole clove
4	reduced-calorie vanilla wafers, crushed
5	tablespoons coarsely chopped pistachios, toasted and divided

Peel and core pears, leaving stems intact. Remove about ¼-inch from base pears so they will sit flat.

Combine water, white wine, sugar, honey, apricots, lemon rind strips, vanilla bean and clove in a large saucepan; bring to a boil. Add pears, cover, reduce heat and simmer until tender, about 10 minutes. Remove pears and apricots from cooking liquid using a slotted spoon. Chill pears and apricots.

Bring cooking liquid to a boil and cook until reduced to 1 cup, about 15 minutes. Strain cooking liquid through a sieve over a bowl and discard solids. Chill.

Chop apricots and combine with wafer crumbs and 1 tablespoon pistachios. Fill each pear with about 2 tablespoons apricot mixture. Place each pear in one of 4 bowls. Spoon ¼ cup syrup over each pear and sprinkle each with 1 tablespoon pistachios.

Calories 251 (22% from fat); fat 6g (sat 0.7g, mono 3.4g, poly 0.9g); protein 3.4g; carb 51.5g; fiber 6.0g.

ACTIVITY – Since 1811, the <u>Bemus Point and Stow Ferry</u> has been a favorite way to cross the beautiful <u>Chautauqua Lake</u>.

Rice Pudding with Raisins

4¾	cups (or more) milk (do not use low-fat or nonfat)
⅔	cup medium- or short-grain white rice
⅓	cup sugar
¼	stick unsalted butter
1	cinnamon stick
	Pinch of salt
⅓	cup golden raisins
2	teaspoons vanilla extract
2	large egg yolks

Combine 4 cups milk, rice, sugar, butter, cinnamon stick and salt in heavy large saucepan. Simmer over medium-low heat until rice is tender and mixture is creamy, stirring frequently, about 1 hour. Remove from heat. Discard cinnamon stick. Stir in raisins and vanilla.

Pour ¾ cup milk into heavy small saucepan. Bring to simmer. Whisk egg yolks in medium bowl to blend. Gradually whisk hot milk into beaten yolks. Return mixture to same saucepan. Stir over medium heat until thermometer registers 160 degrees, about 2 minutes (do not boil). Stir egg mixture into rice mixture.

Transfer rice pudding to large nonmetal bowl. Cover and chill until cold, about 30 minutes. (Can be prepared 1 day ahead. Keep chilled.)

Thin rice pudding with more milk, if desired. Spoon into bowls and serve.

Yield: 6 servings

FITNESS FACT – The top seven healthiest food which are nutrient-rich sources are: prunes, raisins, blueberries, blackberries, kale, strawberries, and spinach.

Winter

Winter

Baked Cheese Sticks

4	cups cornflakes cereal
½	teaspoon dried oregano
1	teaspoon garlic salt
¼	cup all-purpose flour
2	egg whites
2	tablespoons water
1	(8-ounce) package mozzarella cheese

Preheat oven to 400 degrees. Lightly grease a medium baking pan lined with foil.

In a large, shallow bowl, crush the cereal to 1 cup. Mix together the cereal, oregano and garlic salt.

Place the flour in a small bowl.

In another small bowl, thoroughly beat the egg whites and water.

Cut the mozzarella cheese into 12 sticks about 2¾-inches in length. Dip the cheese sticks in the flour, then the egg mixture, then the cereal mixture. Repeat dipping into the egg and cereal mixture to ensure a complete coating. Arrange cheese sticks on the baking pan. Allow the sticks to set for 30 minutes.

Bake 8 minutes or until cheese is soft and sticks are lightly browned.

Yield: 6 servings

ACTIVITY – Buffalo is home to the <u>Sabres</u>, a national hockey team which frequently slashes its way to a top ranking. (Erie)

Garden Veggie Pizza Squares

1 (8-ounce) package refrigerated crescent rolls
1 (8-ounce) package cream cheese, softened
1 (1-ounce) package Ranch-style dressing mix
2 carrots, finely chopped
½ cup chopped sweet red peppers
½ cup chopped bell pepper
½ cup fresh broccoli, chopped
½ cup chopped green onions

Preheat oven to 375 degrees.

Roll out crescent rolls onto a large non-stick cookie sheet. Stretch and flatten to form a single rectangular shape on the cookie sheet. Bake 11-13 minutes in the preheated oven, or until golden brown. Allow to cool.

Place cream cheese in a medium bowl. Mix cream cheese with ½ of the ranch dressing mix. Adjust the amount of dressing mix to taste. Spread the mixture over the cooled crust. Arrange carrot, sweet red pepper, bell pepper, broccoli and green onions on top. Chill in refrigerator about 1 hour. Cut into bite-size squares to serve.

Yield: 24 servings

FUN FACT – The Winter Solstice is December 22, the longest night of the year.

Spanakopita

1	stick (½ cup) plus 1 tablespoon unsalted butter
1	pound baby spinach
½	teaspoon salt
½	teaspoon pepper
½	pound feta, crumbled (scant 2 cups)
½	teaspoon freshly grated nutmeg
10	(17 x 12-inch) phyllo sheets, thawed if frozen

Melt 1 tablespoon butter in a 12-inch heavy skillet over moderate heat, then cook spinach, stirring, until wilted and tender, about 4 minutes. Remove from heat and cool, about 10 minutes. Squeeze handfuls of spinach to remove as much liquid as possible, then coarsely chop. Transfer to a bowl and stir in feta, nutmeg, ½ teaspoon salt, and ½ teaspoon pepper.

Preheat oven to 375 degrees.

Melt remaining stick of butter in a small saucepan, then cool.

Cover phyllo stack with 2 overlapping sheets of plastic wrap and then a dampened kitchen towel. Take 1 phyllo sheet from stack and arrange on a work surface with a long side nearest you (keeping remaining sheets covered) and brush with some butter. Top with another phyllo sheet and brush with more butter. Cut buttered phyllo stack crosswise into 6 (roughly 12 x 2¾-inch) strips.

Put a heaping teaspoon of filling near 1 corner of a strip on end nearest you, then fold corner of phyllo over to enclose filling and form a triangle. Continue folding strip (like a flag), maintaining triangle shape. Put triangle, seam side down, on a large cookie sheet and brush top with butter. Make more triangles in same manner, using all of phyllo.

Bake in middle of oven 20-25 minutes or until golden brown, then transfer to a rack to cool slightly.

Pastry triangles can be formed, but not baked, 3 days ahead. Arrange in 1 layer in heavy-duty sealed plastic bags, then freeze. Bake frozen pastries (do not thaw) in same manner as above.

Yield: 30 servings

ACTIVITY – Buffalo houses a major football team, the Buffalo Bills, in Orchard Park. They have an ongoing rivalry with the New York Jets at the other end of the state. (Erie)

Jeannine's Veggie-Cream Cheese Spread

1   (8-ounce) package reduced fat
    cream cheese at room
    temperature

1   teaspoon crushed or powdered
    garlic

3   tablespoons green onions, finely
    chopped

3   tablespoons green bell pepper,
    finely chopped

3   tablespoons carrot, grated

In a medium-sized mixing bowl combine cream cheese and garlic and beat with electric mixer until smooth.

Stir in green onions, pepper and carrots with a wooden spoon. Transfer to a covered container and chill for at least 2 hours or up to 1 day before serving.

Serve with whole grain or wheat crackers or use as filling for finger sandwiches.

FITNESS FACT – Each exercise session should include a warm-up, the dynamic exercise, and a cool-down period.

Cheese and Garlic Fondue

1   pound Swiss cheese, grated
½   cup Gruyère cheese, grated
3   tablespoons all-purpose flour
1   teaspoon ground nutmeg
½   teaspoon ground white pepper
1¼   cups dry white wine
3   large garlic cloves, minced
1   pound crusty French bread or
        sourdough bread, cut into
        1½-inch cubes

Combine both cheeses, flour, nutmeg, and white pepper in large bowl; toss to coat.

Bring 1 cup wine and garlic to simmer in a heavy large saucepan over low heat. Add cheese mixture by handfuls, whisking until melted and smooth after each addition. Mix in more wine by tablespoonfuls to reach desired consistency. Transfer to fondue pot.

Set fondue over candle or canned heat. Serve fondue with bread and skewers or long forks for dipping.

ACTIVITY – The Ansley Wilcox Mansion in Buffalo was the site of Theodore Roosevelt's swearing in as President of the United States after the death of President William McKinley from an assassin's bullet. The mansion is the site today of such events as the "Teddy Bear Picnic" in August and the "Victorian Christmas" in December.

Spinach Artichoke Dip

2	(8-ounce) packages cream cheese, room temperature
⅓	cup sour cream
¼	cup mayonnaise
1	tablespoon fresh lemon juice
1	tablespoon Dijon mustard
1	garlic clove, minced
1	teaspoon Worcestershire sauce
½	teaspoon hot pepper sauce
3	(6-ounce) jars marinated artichoke hearts, drained, coarsely chopped
1	cup grated mozzarella or sharp Cheddar cheese or a mixture of the cheeses
3	green onions, finely chopped
2	teaspoons minced seeded jalapeño chili
6	(6-inch) pita rounds, each cut into 6 triangles
	Olive oil

Preheat oven to 400 degrees.

Using electric mixer, beat cream cheese, sour cream, mayonnaise, lemon juice, mustard, garlic, Worcestershire sauce and hot pepper sauce in large bowl to blend. Fold in artichokes, mozzarella or sharp Cheddar cheese, green onions and jalapeño. Transfer to 11 x 7 x 2-inch glass baking dish. (Can be made 1 day ahead. Cover and refrigerate.)

Place pita triangles in single layer on cookie sheet and brush with oil, sprinkle with salt. Bake, about 10 minutes or until crisp and remove from oven. Maintain oven temperature and bake dip about 20 minutes or until bubbling and brown on top. Serve hot dip with pita chips.

FUN FACT – You can pour olive oil into a clean, empty container, cover and freeze and when it is very cold and thick, use as a spread for bread.

Frosted Grapes and Cheese Platter

2   large egg whites
10   small clusters of seedless grapes
      (a mixture of colors is
      especially nice).
      Granulated sugar, enough will be
      needed to completely cover the
      grapes

Place a large rack (make sure grapes will not fall through) on top of a sheet of aluminum foil. Whisk egg whites in medium bowl until frothy. Dip grape clusters into egg whites to coat arrange clusters on rack and sift sugar over grapes, turning the grapes by holding the stems to coat on all sides. Let grapes stand until dry, at least 2 hours and up to 8 hours.

Arrange frosted grapes on a platter with 3 or 4 assorted cheese wedges (Sharp Cheddar, Roquefort, Camembert, Brie, Gorgonzola) and crackers or toasts.

ACTIVITY – The Arcade and Attica Railroad, (Wyoming) is a steam passenger excursion – a rare find today. Special events include war enactments, costumed children characters, holiday themes and murder mystery.

Armadillo Eggs

24	jalapeño peppers
1	pound sausage
2	cups all-purpose baking mix
1	(16-ounce) package Cheddar cheese, shredded
1	tablespoon crushed red pepper flakes
1	tablespoon garlic salt
1	(16-ounce) package Monterey Jack cheese, cubed

Preheat oven to 325 degrees. Lightly grease a medium cookie sheet.

Cut a slit in each jalapeño pepper. Remove and discard seeds and pulp.

In a medium bowl, mix sausage, baking mix, Cheddar cheese, crushed red pepper and garlic salt.

Stuff jalapeños with Monterey Jack cheese cubes. Shape sausage mixture around the jalapeños to form balls.

Arrange jalapeño balls on the prepared cookie sheet. Bake 25 minutes or until lightly browned.

Yield: 12 servings

FUN FACT – If you rub a wooden cutting board or chopping block with a few drops of oil it will preserve it as well as prevent food from sticking to it.

Quick Chili Soup

1	can tomato soup
1	(8-ounce) can French onion soup
2	cups water
1	(16-ounce) can garbanzo beans drained and rinsed
1	(16-ounce) can black beans, drained and rinsed
1	(16-ounce) can refried beans
1	tablespoon chili powder
½	teaspoon cumin powder
½	teaspoon dried thyme

Combine all ingredients. Heat to boiling over medium heat. Turn heat to low and simmer for 40 minutes.

ACTIVITY – Snow permitting, Erie County's Winter Carnival is held at various parks during the selected weekends. Activities include ice carving, pony rides, winter sports, model airplane demos, snow mobile and hayrides.

Cream of Vegetable Soup

2 cups cooked vegetables of your choice
1 cup onions, chopped
1 tablespoon parsley, chopped
4 cups chicken or vegetable stock
1 cup heavy cream
  Salt and pepper to taste

Put the vegetables, parsley and stock in a saucepan; bring to a boil. Lower the heat and simmer, partially covered, for 10-15 minutes or until vegetables are tender. In a blender, food mill or food processor purée the soup until it is as smooth as you like.

Return the purée to the saucepan and add the cream. To serve cold, chill for at least 2 hours and correct seasoning, as needed. To serve hot, keep heating soup and stirring until mixture is heated through. Season as needed.

Some vegetable combinations to try: Leeks (omit onion and use 3 cups leeks and teaspoon fresh tarragon). Onions: use 3 cups onion. Potatoes: use 2 cups diced onion, 5 cups chicken stock, 2 teaspoons fresh dill and sour cream. Mushrooms: use 2 teaspoons chopped fresh savory. Celery: use 1 teaspoon chopped fresh sage. Cauliflower: use a dash of nutmeg. Tomato: use 1 tablespoon chopped fresh basil.

FUN FACT – The Campbell Soup Company reports that they make more pasta stars than there are real stars in the Milky Way.

Cream of Celery Soup

4	cups celery, 1-inch chunks
3	cups potatoes, 1-inch chunks
4	cups water
1	teaspoon salt
1	cup minced onion
1	cup celery, very finely minced
¼	teaspoon celery seeds
¼	teaspoon salt
2	tablespoons butter
1	cup milk
¼	cup sour cream or heavy cream
	White pepper, to taste

Bring celery and potato chunks, water, and salt to a boil in a saucepan. Reduce heat, partially cover pan and cook until soft. Purée in blender. Return to pan.

Sauté onion with salt in butter until translucent. Add celery and celery seed. Sauté until tender. Add to first mixture. Whisk milk, sour or heavy cream and white pepper into soup about 10 minutes before serving. Heat the soup gently, don't boil. Serve as soon as it's hot.

ACTIVITY – <u>First Night Buffalo</u> is a family celebration of New Year's Eve.

Curried Corn and Shrimp Soup

2 cups regular-strength chicken broth
2 medium-sized tart apples, peeled, cored and chopped
1 large onion, chopped
½ teaspoon curry powder
1 large red bell pepper, stemmed and seeded
4 cups cold buttermilk
¼ cup lime juice
1½ cups cooked corn kernels
½ cup minced fresh cilantro
⅓ pound tiny cooked shrimp
Cilantro sprigs (optional)

In a 4-5 quart pan combine broth, apples, onion, and curry. Cover and bring to a boil, then simmer until apples mash easily (about 30 minutes). Let cool, then cover and chill until cold, at least 3 hours or up to a day. Smoothly purée mixture in a blender or food processor.

Cut a few thin slivers from bell pepper and set aside; dice remaining pepper and put into a tureen with apple purée, buttermilk, lime juice, 1¼ cups of corn and minced cilantro. Ladle soup into bowls and top with shrimp, remaining corn, bell pepper strips, and cilantro sprigs.

FUN FACT – Mineral residue on pots can be cleaned by soaking with white vinegar before washing.

Beef Vegetable Soup

1   cup dried porcini mushrooms
3   (13¼-ounce) cans beef broth
1   teaspoon olive oil
1   pound beef top round steak cut
       into 1¼ x ¼ x ¼-inch strips
2   cloves garlic, pressed
1   cup frozen small whole onions
1   (16-ounce) can diced tomatoes
1   (10-ounce) package frozen green
       peas

Combine the mushrooms and 1 can of beef broth in a small bowl. Let stand 30 minutes for mushrooms to soften. Heat oil in a 4-quart saucepan or 5-quart Dutch oven over medium-high heat. Add beef and stir fry 1-2 minutes. Remove beef to a bowl and keep warm. Add garlic to pot and cook stirring constantly for 1 minute. Drain mushrooms reserving broth. Chop mushrooms and reserve. Add reserved broth to saucepan along with remaining 2 cans of broth. Bring to boiling and add onions. Return to boiling and cook 3 minutes. Add tomatoes, green peas, reserved beef and mushrooms. Return to boiling. Reduce heat to low and simmer for 5 minutes.

Yield: 4 servings

ACTIVITY – <u>Architectural Tours</u>: Houses of Worship provide a chance to see Buffalo's nationally recognized churches and temples, so rich in history, design and heritage.

Simple Split Pea Soup

2	tablespoons (¼ stick) butter
1	large onion, chopped
1	cup chopped celery
1	cup chopped peeled carrots
1½	pounds smoked pork hocks
2	teaspoons dried leaf marjoram
1½	cups green split peas
8	cups water
	Salt and pepper to taste

Melt butter in heavy large pot or Dutch oven over medium-high heat. Add onion, celery and carrots, sauté until vegetables begin to soften, about 8 minutes. Add pork hocks and marjoram; stir 1 minute. Add peas and water; bring to boil. Reduce heat to medium-low and partially cover pot. Simmer until pork and vegetables are tender (peas will start falling apart) stirring often, about 1 hour and 10 minutes. Remove hocks from pot and place into a large bowl.

Purée 5 cups soup in batches in blender or food processor and return to pot. Cut pork off hocks, dice and return to soup. Season with salt and pepper to taste.

Can be made 1 day ahead – refrigerate until cold, then cover – rewarm before serving.

FITNESS FACT – The average calories spent cross-country skiing by a 150-pound person are 700 calories per hour. A lighter person burns fewer calories; a heavier person burns more.

24-Hour Vegetable Salad

4   cups torn iceberg, romaine,
       spinach, leaf and/or Bibb,
       lettuce

     Salt and pepper to taste

1   cup sliced mushrooms

1   cup broccoli florets and/or frozen
       peas

1   cup shredded carrots

2   hard-cooked eggs, sliced

6   slices, bacon, cooked and
       crumbled

¾   cup shredded Swiss or Cheddar
       cheese

¼   cup thinly sliced green onions

¾   cup mayonnaise or salad
       dressing

1½ teaspoons lemon juice

½   teaspoon dried dill (optional)

Place lettuce in a 3-quart salad bowl. If desired, sprinkle with salt and pepper. Layer atop lettuce in the following order: mushrooms, broccoli, and/or peas, carrots, eggs, bacon, ½ cup cheese and green onions.

In a small bowl for dressing combine the mayonnaise or salad dressing, lemon juice, and dill, if desired. Spread dressing over top of salad.

Sprinkle with remaining ¼ cup cheese. Cover and chill for 2-24 hours. Before serving, toss to coat vegetables.

ACTIVITY – Buffalo Museum of Science and Kellogg Observatory (Erie) – Opened in 1915, this Museum's collection concentrates on life in the Greater Niagara Region in anthropology, botany, entomology, mycology, paleontology and zoology. The first museum in the nation to house an elementary school on site and be incorporated within the curriculum.

Crab Salad

1	cup mayonnaise
¼	cup heavy cream
½	cup chili sauce
2	tablespoons chopped green olives
1	teaspoon prepared horseradish
1	teaspoon Worcester sauce
2	green onions, chopped fine
1	tablespoon lemon juice
1	pound crabmeat
	Crisp lettuce
	Chopped parsley or chives
1	tomato, quartered
1	hard-cooked egg, quartered

Prepare dressing by combining the first 8 ingredients.

Arrange the crabmeat in a bed of crisp lettuce. Cover with dressing and garnish with the chopped parsley or chives.

Arrange quartered tomatoes and quartered hard-cooked eggs around symmetrically.

FUN FACT – The word onion is derived from a Latin word which means large pearl.

Club Salad

12 cups salad greens
4   cups cooked, cubed turkey, ham and/or chicken
2   avocados, peeled and cubed
2   ounces bleu cheese, crumbled
5   green onions, sliced

Dressing
1   cup yogurt
1   cup sour cream
1   package dry ranch dressing mix
1   cup mayonnaise

Garnish
8   slices bacon, crumbled
4   hard-cooked eggs, chopped
1   basket cherry tomatoes

Layer greens, meat, avocado, bleu cheese, and onion in a deep glass salad bowl.

Combine all dressing ingredients in a medium bowl. Spread dressing over salad.

Garnish with bacon, eggs, and cherry tomatoes.

ACTIVITY – <u>Cut your own perfect, fresh and fragrant Christmas trees</u> from select farms in Orleans, Genesee, Erie, and Wyoming counties for a memorable holiday tradition.

No-Fat Tuna Salad

1	tablespoon Grey Poupon mustard
1	tablespoon hot and sweet mustard
	Black pepper or Tabasco to taste
1	tablespoon lemon juice
1	cup nonfat sour cream
1	(8-ounce) can water-packed albacore tuna
1	cup minced carrots
½	cup minced bell pepper
½	cup minced onion
1	cup minced celery
¼	cup minced fresh dill or parsley

Add the mustards, pepper, and lemon juice to the sour cream. Add the remaining ingredients and mix well.

Yield: 6 servings

FITNESS FACT – Studies have shown that exercise can be split into shorter segments (10 minutes, 2-3 times daily) and still reap the same health benefits as one longer segment (20-30 minutes, all at once) can.

Sweet Apple Quick Bread

2	cups flour
1	cup sugar
1	teaspoon baking soda
½	teaspoon baking powder
1	cup apples, peeled and finely chopped
8	tablespoons butter, softened
½	cup milk
2	tablespoons orange peel, grated
1	tablespoon corn syrup
2	eggs
½	cup chopped nuts

Blend all ingredients except nuts. Beat 3 minutes then fold in nuts. Pour into greased loaf pan. Bake at 325 degrees for 50-60 minutes or until toothpick comes out clean. Remove from pan to cool.

ACTIVITY – The World's Largest Disco is held in Buffalo. Come dance on New York State's largest dance floor and be a part of the largest Retro party in the world! Have fun while also contributing to local charities!

Brown Bread

2	pounds wheat flour
1	pound self-raising flour
1	ounces coarse bran
2	ounces wheat germ
2	teaspoons baking soda
1	teaspoon salt
2	ounces brown sugar
4	ounces butter
2	large eggs
1¾	pints buttermilk

Preheat oven to 425 degrees.

Mix all dry ingredients. Rub or cut in butter with pastry blender. Whisk eggs into buttermilk. Add liquid to dry mix. Mix thoroughly until nice and soft. Shape into 2 loaves. Brush with milk, cut across top diagonally 3-4 times.

Put on pizza stone or greased baking sheet sprinkled with cornmeal. Reduce heat to 400 degrees, bake 40-45 minutes or until top is nicely browned and bread sounds hollow when tapped on bottom. Otherwise, turn over and bake additional 5 minutes.

FITNESS FACT – Lack of exercise does make the muscles shrink, reducing the body's calorie-burning rate. The lack of activity itself further reduces the number of calories you burn.

German Rye Bread

1	(¼-ounce) package active dry yeast
4	cups warm water (110-155 degrees), divided
2	cups rye flour
6	tablespoons sugar
2	tablespoons caraway seeds
2	teaspoons salt
7-8	cups all-purpose flour
2	teaspoons cornmeal

Topping

1	egg
4	teaspoons caraway seeds

In a 4-quart class bowl, dissolve yeast in 2 cups of warm water; whisk in rye flour until smooth. Cover loosely with a clean kitchen towel. Let stand in a warm place for about 4 hours or until batter falls about 1-inch and surface bubble activity is reduced. Stir in the sugar, caraway seeds, salt, 5 cups all-purpose flour and remaining water; mix well. Stir in enough remaining flour to form a firm dough. Turn onto a floured surface; knead until smooth and elastic, about 8 minutes. Cover and let rest for 15 minutes.

Divide dough into 4 portions. Cover and let rest for 15 minutes. Shape into 4 round loaves, about 6-inches each. Coat 2 baking sheets with nonstick cooking spray; sprinkle each with 1 teaspoon cornmeal. Place loaves on pans. Cover and let rise until doubled, about 45 minutes.

With a shape knife, make several slashes across the top of each loaf. Brush with egg. Sprinkle each loaf with 1 teaspoon caraway seeds. Bake at 400 degrees for 30-35 minutes, or until browned. Rotate pans after 15 minutes of baking. Cool on wire racks.

Yield: 4 loaves (8 slices each)

ACTIVITY – Herschell Carousel Factory Museum in North Tonawanda. The Carousel Museum is actually housed in a carousel factory building.

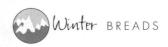

Jam-Filled Muffins

2   cups all-purpose (plain) flour
¾   cup sugar
1   tablespoon baking powder
½   teaspoon baking soda
½   teaspoon salt
6   tablespoons unsalted butter, melted
2   large eggs
1   teaspoon vanilla extract
¼   teaspoon almond extract
1¼   cups sour cream
⅓-½ cup jelly or seedless jam (red currant jelly or raspberry, blackberry or strawberry jam)

Preheat the oven to 375 degrees. Grease 12 standard muffin cups with butter or butter-flavored nonstick cooking spray.

In a bowl, stir together flour, sugar, baking powder, baking soda and salt. In another bowl, whisk together the melted butter, eggs, vanilla and almond extracts and sour cream until smooth. Add the egg mixture to the dry ingredients and stir just until evenly moistened. The batter will be slightly lumpy. Do not over mix. Spoon the batter into each muffin cup, filling it ⅓ full.

Drop a heaping teaspoonful of jelly or jam into the center, cover with batter level with the rim of the cup.

Bake until golden, dry and springy to the touch, 20-25 minutes. Transfer the pan to a wire rack and let cool for 5 minutes. Unmold the muffins. Serve warm or at room temperature.

Yield: 12 muffins

FUN FACT – The rose family of plants, in addition to flowers, gives us apples, pears, plums, cherries, almonds, peaches and apricots.

Lemon -Anise Biscotti

2 cups unbleached all-purpose flour
1 teaspoon baking powder
¼ teaspoon salt
1 cup sugar
2 large eggs
¼ teaspoon vanilla extract
1 tablespoon zest from 1 lemon
1 tablespoon anise seed

Sift flour, baking powder and salt in small bowl. Whisk sugar and eggs in large bowl to a light lemon color, stir in vanilla, lemon zest and anise seed. Sift dry ingredients over egg mixture then fold in until dough is just combined.

Adjust oven rack to middle position and heat oven to 350 degrees. Half dough and turn each portion onto an oiled cookie sheet covered with parchment. Using floured hands, quickly stretch each portion of dough into a rough 13 x 2-inch log, placing them about 3-inches apart on the cookie sheet. Pat each dough shape and smooth it.

Bake, turning pan once, until loaves are golden and just beginning to crack on top, about 35 minutes. Cool the loaves for 10 minutes; lower oven temperature to 325 degrees.

Cut each loaf diagonally into ⅜-inch slices with a serrated knife. Lay the slices about ½-inch apart on the cookie sheet, cut side up, and return them to the oven. Bake, turning over each cookie halfway through baking, until crisp and golden brown on both sides, about 15 minutes. Transfer biscotti to wire rack and cool completely. Biscotti can be stored in an airtight container for at least 1 month.

Follow the mixing, baking and slicing instructions for Lemon-Anise Biscotti, substituting ⅓ cup of unhulled sesame seeds for the anise seeds in the recipe. Brush the top of each loaf of dough with an egg wash and sprinkle the additional sesame seeds.

Yield: 3-4 dozen

ACTIVITY – Niagara University is home to the Castellani Art Museum which specializes in twentieth century art.

Hearty Lentil and Mushroom Loaf with Potato Filling

1   cup raw lentils
1   tablespoon canola oil
2   cloves garlic, minced
2   ounces white or brown
     mushrooms
5   ounces (half a package) thawed
     frozen spinach
1   tablespoon soy sauce
2   tablespoons wheat germ
     Fresh ground pepper to taste
⅛   teaspoon nutmeg
1   cup firmly packed Stilton or
     Gruyère cheese (Stilton is a
     much stronger cheese)
     Cooking spray

Filling

1   tablespoon canola oil
1   cup chopped onion
¼   cup dry bread crumbs
1   cup coarsely mashed potato
     (about 1 medium cooked
     potato, peeling optional)
½   teaspoon salt
½   teaspoon dried thyme
½   teaspoon dried basil
     Fresh ground pepper to taste
     Curly parsley for garnish
     (optional)

Rinse and strain lentils to remove any debris. In a heavy sauce pan combine lentils with 4 cups water and bring to a boil. Lower heat and simmer covered until tender, about 45 minutes.

Preheat oven to 350 degrees.

In a large skillet heat oil, then add garlic and mushrooms and sauté over medium heat until mushrooms are wilted. Stir in the spinach, lentils, soy sauce and wheat germ. Cook, stirring until mixture is completely heated and then add cheese.

Coat the inside of a 9 x 5 x 3-inch loaf pan with cooking spray (glass is preferable). Press ⅔ of the lentil mixture evenly into the sides and bottom of loaf pan to form a shell. Set the remaining ⅓ of the lentil mixture aside

Filling: Using a clean skillet heat oil, then add onion and sauté until golden brown. Add to onion, bread crumbs, potato, salt, thyme, basil and pepper to taste and sauté, stirring occasionally, for 5 minutes. Add filling to lentil shell and cover with remaining lentil mixture. Bake at 350 degrees until crusty, about 40-45 minutes. Remove from oven and let stand for 15 minutes. Loosen edges of loaf from pan with a knife or spatula. Slice and serve with curly parsley garnish.

FUN FACTS – Each American eats approximately 22 pounds of tomatoes yearly. Over one-half of the tomato consumptions is in the form of catsup and tomato sauce.

Pinto Bean Stew

1	cup dry pinto beans
2	cups cold water
½	cup chopped carrot
2	garlic cloves, minced
¾	teaspoon chili powder
½	teaspoon salt
	Dash cayenne pepper
1	(16-ounce) package frozen corn, thawed
1	large onion, chopped
1	medium-sized green pepper, chopped
1	(14½-ounce) can diced tomatoes, undrained
2-3	teaspoons balsamic vinegar
¼	teaspoon sugar

Place beans in a large saucepan; add water to cover by 2-inches. Bring to boil; boil for 2 minutes. Remove from heat; cover and let stand for 1 hour. Drain and rinse beans, discarding liquid. Return beans to pan; add cold water, carrot, garlic, chili powder, salt and cayenne. Bring to boil. Reduce heat; cover and simmer for 45 minutes or until beans are almost tender.

In a nonstick skillet coated with nonstick cooking spray; sauté the corn, onion and green pepper until tender. Add to the bean mixture. Cover and cook for 45 minutes. Stir in the tomatoes, vinegar and sugar. Cook 5 minutes longer or until heated through.

Yield: 6 servings

One serving (1 cup) equals 214 calories, 1 gram fat (trace saturated fat), 0 cholesterol, 309 milligrams sodium, 45 grams carbohydrate, 10 grams fiber, 10 grams protein. Diabetic Exchanges: 2 starch, 1 very lean meat, 1 vegetable.

ACTIVITY – Allegheny State Park, Salamanca (Cattaraugus) – is the largest park in the New York State system. It has over 35 miles of cross-country ski trails.

Shrimp Creole Style

1   large onion, chopped
½   cup finely chopped green pepper
1   celery rib with leaves, finely chopped
1   tablespoon canola oil
3   garlic cloves, minced
1   (28-ounce) can whole tomatoes
¼   cup minced fresh parsley
¼   cup water
¼   cup tomato paste
2   tablespoons lime juice
1   teaspoon dried thyme
¾   teaspoon salt
½   teaspoon dried oregano
¼-½ teaspoon hot pepper sauce
¼   teaspoon ground allspice
36   cooked large shrimp, peeled and deveined

In a large nonstick skillet, sauté the onion, green pepper and celery in oil for 3-4 minutes. Add garlic; cook 1 minute longer. Drain tomatoes, reserving juice; add juice to skillet. Mash tomatoes and add to skillet. Stir in the parsley and next 8 ingredients. Bring to boil. Reduce heat; simmer, uncovered, for 15 minutes or until thickened. Serve warm with shrimp.

Yield: 12 servings

FITNESS FACT – As the cold and flu season kicks into high gear this winter, it's good to know that regular exercise may be your first line of defense. Being active may actually reduce the number of colds people get each year. The key is to strike the right balance between exercise, good nutrition and adequate sleep.

Marinated Orange Roughy

1½ pounds orange roughy or other whitefish fillets
½   cup orange juice
¼   cup ketchup
2   tablespoons canola oil
2   tablespoons reduced-sodium soy sauce
2   tablespoons lemon juice
¼   teaspoon pepper
1   tablespoon sesame seeds, toasted

Cut fillets into 4 pieces if necessary; set aside. In a bowl, combine the orange juice, ketchup, oil, soy sauce, lemon juice and pepper; mix well. Remove ¼ cup for basting; cover and refrigerate. Pour remaining marinade into a large re-sealable plastic bag; add fillets. Seal bag and turn to coat; refrigerate for 2 hours, turning once or twice.

Drain fillets and discard marinade. Place fillets on a broiler pan coated with nonstick cooking spray. Broil 4-6 inches from the heat for 5-6 minutes on each side or until fish flakes easily with a fork, basting occasionally with reserved marinade. Sprinkle with sesame seeds.

Yield: 4 servings

One serving equals 181 calories, 5 grams fat (trace saturated fat), 34 milligrams cholesterol, 349 milligrams sodium, 4 grams carbohydrate, trace fiber, 25 grams protein. Diabetic Exchanges: 4 very lean meat, 1 fat.

ACTIVITY – The Burchfield-Penney Art Center, Buffalo (Erie) – contains a great collection of regional art, centered on the works of Charles Burchfield, best known for his watercolors.

Turkey Manicotti

¼ cup bulgur*
⅔ cup boiling water
¾ pound lean ground turkey
1½ cups 2% small-curd cottage cheese
1 teaspoon dried basil
1 teaspoon dried oregano
½ teaspoon salt
¼ teaspoon pepper
14 uncooked manicotti shells
1 (28-ounce) jar meatless spaghetti sauce
½ cup water
1 (4-ounce) cup shredded part-skim mozzarella cheese

Place the bulgur in a bowl; stir in boiling water. Cover and let stand for 30 minutes or until the liquid is absorbed. Drain and squeeze dry.

In a nonstick skillet, cook turkey over medium heat until no longer pink; drain. Add the cottage cheese, basil, oregano, salt, pepper and bulgur; mix well. Stuff into uncooked manicotti shells. Arrange in a 13 x 9 x 2-inch baking dish coated with nonstick cooking spray.

Combine spaghetti sauce and water; pour over shells. Cover and bake at 350 degrees for 1 hour, 15 minutes or until shells are tender and sauce is bubbly. Uncover; sprinkle with mozzarella cheese. Bake 5 minutes longer or until cheese is melted.

Yield: 7 servings

One serving (2 stuffed shells) equals 418 calories, 13 grams fat (5 grams saturated fat), 51 milligrams cholesterol, 986 milligrams sodium, 49 grams carbohydrate, 6 grams fiber, 27 grams protein. Diabetic Exchanges: 3 lean meat, 3 starch, ½ fat.

*Look for bulgur in the cereal, rice or organic food aisle of your grocery store.

TRIVIA – Eat Like A Bird? Every day, birds eat one-half their own weight in food! So, why do people say that a poor eater "eats like a bird"? If this were the case, a 50 pound child would consume 25 pounds of food a day!

Asparagus Ham Dinner

2	cups uncooked spiral pasta
¾	pound fresh asparagus, cut into 1-inch pieces
1	medium yellow pepper, julienne
1	tablespoon olive or canola oil
3	cups diced fresh tomatoes (about 6 medium)
6	ounces reduced-sodium fully cooked ham, cubed
¼	cup minced fresh parsley
½	teaspoon salt
½	teaspoon dried oregano
½	teaspoon dried basil
⅛-¼	teaspoon cayenne pepper
	Parmesan cheese

Cook pasta according to package directions. Meanwhile, in a nonstick skillet, sauté asparagus and yellow pepper in oil until tender. Add tomatoes and ham; heat through. Drain pasta; add to the vegetable mixture. Stir in seasonings. Sprinkle with Parmesan cheese.

Yield: 6 servings

One serving (1 ⅓ cups) equals 238 calories, 6 grams fat (1 gram saturated fat), 18 milligrams cholesterol, 522 milligrams sodium, 33 grams carbohydrate, 3 grams fiber, 14 grams protein. Diabetic Exchanges: 2 lean meat, 2 vegetables, 1 starch.

ACTIVITY – The Pierce-Arrow Museum, Buffalo (Erie) – is located near downtown Buffalo. It contains a vast collection of cars and motoring memorabilia from before 1940.

Flavorful White Chili

1	pound dry great Northern beans, rinsed and sorted
4	cups chicken broth
2	cups chopped onions
3	garlic cloves, minced
2	teaspoons ground cumin
1½	teaspoons dried oregano
1	teaspoon ground coriander
⅛	teaspoon ground cloves
⅛	teaspoon cayenne pepper
1	(4-ounce) can chopped green chilies
½	pound boneless skinless chicken breast, grilled and cubed
1	teaspoon salt
¾	cup shredded reduced-fat Mexican cheese blend

Place beans in a soup kettle or Dutch oven; add water to cover by 2-inches. Bring to boil; boil for 2 minutes. Remove from heat; cover and let stand 1 hour. Drain and rinse beans, discarding liquid.

Place beans in a slow cooker. Add broth and the next 7 ingredients. Cover and cook on low for 7-8 hours or until beans are almost tender. Add the chilies, chicken and salt; cover and cook 1 hour or until beans are tender. Serve with cheese.

Yield: 6 servings

One serving (1⅓ cups chili with 2 tablespoons cheese) equals 384 calories, 5 grams fat (2 grams saturated fat), 37 milligrams cholesterol, 1,224 milligrams sodium, 53 grams carbohydrate, 16 grams fiber, 34 grams protein. Diabetic Exchanges: 4 very lean meat, 3 starch.

FUN FACT – Thyme is sweet, yet pungent. Use with poultry and fish, add to stuffings or meatloaf. Good with most vegetables, especially potatoes, carrots, squash, onions and tomatoes.

Beef Tenderloin with Beaujolais

2¼ pounds beef tenderloin

5 teaspoons minced fresh thyme, divided

1 teaspoon salt

½ teaspoon coarsely ground pepper

½ cup dried porcini mushrooms (about ½-ounce)

1 (750-milliliter) bottle Beaujolais or other light, fruity red wine (use a good quality wine)

1 (14¼-ounce) can fat-free beef broth

2 garlic cloves, minced

1 tablespoon water

2 teaspoons cornstarch

1 teaspoon olive oil

Cooking spray

Preheat oven to 400 degrees.

Trim fat from the tenderloin and combine 3 teaspoons thyme, salt, and pepper; rub evenly over tenderloin. Cover and chill 2 hours.

Combine 2 teaspoons thyme, mushrooms, wine, broth, and garlic in a large saucepan, and bring to a boil. Reduce heat, and simmer until reduced to 1½ cups (about 1 hour). Combine water and cornstarch, and stir into wine mixture. Bring to a boil, and cook 1 minute, stirring constantly. Remove wine mixture from heat; set aside, and keep warm.

Heat oil in a large nonstick skillet over medium-high heat. Add tenderloin, browning on all sides, about 12 minutes. Place tenderloin on a broiler pan coated with cooking spray. Insert meat thermometer into thickest portion of tenderloin. Bake at 400 degrees for 20 minutes or until thermometer registers 130 degrees (medium-rare) to 150 degrees (medium). Place tenderloin on a serving platter, and cover with foil. Let stand for 10 minutes. Serve with Beaujolais jus.

8 servings (serving size: 3 ounces beef and 3 tablespoons au jus) calories 201 (39% from fat); fat 8.6g (sat 3.2g) protein 25.7g; carbohydrates 3.7g; fiber 0.3g

ACTIVITY – Adams Art Gallery, Dunkirk (Chautauqua) – provides classes, lectures and exhibitions for children and adults. A wide range of art is displayed including mixed media and monotypes.

Beef Sirloin and Vegetables

1   tablespoon cornstarch
1   teaspoon reduced-sodium beef
        bouillon granules
1   cup water
¼   cup reduced-sodium soy sauce
10 ounces boneless beef sirloin steak
1   medium green pepper, julienne
1   medium onion, halved and sliced
1   garlic clove, minced
2   teaspoons canola oil
2   medium tomatoes cut into eighths
1   (8-ounce) can sliced water
        chestnuts, drained
⅛   teaspoon pepper
4   cups hot cooked rice

In a bowl, combine cornstarch, bouillon, water and soy sauce; set aside. Cut steak thinly across the grain, then cut slices in half; set aside. In a nonstick skillet or wok, stir-fry green pepper, onion and garlic in oil for 4 minutes; remove and set aside. Add meat; stir-fry for 4-6 minutes.

Stir cornstarch mixture and add to pan. Bring to boil; cook and stir for 1 minute or until thickened. Add tomatoes, water chestnuts and green pepper mixture; cook and stir until heated through. Sprinkle with pepper. Serve over rice.

Yield: 4 servings

One serving (1½ cups meat mixture with 1 cup rice) equals 469 calories, 15 grams fat (5 grams saturated fat), 46 milligrams cholesterol, 678 milligrams sodium, 62 grams carbohydrate, 5 grams fiber, 21 grams protein. Diabetic Exchanges: 3 lean meat, 2 vegetables, 2 starch, 2 fat.

TRIVIA – Did you know there are over 15,000 varieties of rice?

Halftime Chili

2	tablespoons olive oil
1½	cups chopped onions
8	large garlic cloves, chopped
3	pounds ground chuck
5	tablespoons chili powder
1	tablespoon ground cumin
1	teaspoon dried basil
½	teaspoon dried oregano
½	teaspoon dried thyme
1	(28-ounce) can crushed tomatoes with added purée
1	(14½-ounce) low salt chicken broth
1	(12-ounce) bottle beer
1	(6-ounce) can tomato paste
1	(15 to 16-ounce) can prepared chili beans
	Salt
	Ground pepper

Heat oil in heavy large Dutch oven over medium-high heat. Add onions and garlic.

Sauté onion until translucent, about 8 minutes. Add ground chuck and sauté until brown, breaking up meat with back of spoon, about 5 minutes. Add chili powder, cumin, basil, oregano and thyme. Stir 2 minutes.

Mix in crushed tomatoes, chicken broth, beer and tomato paste. Simmer until thickened to desired consistency, stirring occasionally to prevent sticking, about 1 hour, 15 minutes. Mix in beans. Simmer 5 minutes. Season to taste with salt and pepper.

Can be prepared 3 days ahead. Refrigerate until cold, then cover. Reheat over low heat before serving.

Yield: 8-10 servings

ACTIVITY – Bond Lake County Park, Lewiston (Niagara) – Trails are located along the Lake and through fruit orchards. The Park also offers an ice skating rink and sledding hill.

Italian Vegetables

1	medium carrot, cut into ¼-inch slices
½	cup water
1	cup broccoli florets
1	medium onion, cut into 16 wedges
1	medium zucchini, cut into ¼-inch slices
¼	cup fat-free Italian salad dressing
¼	teaspoon dried oregano

In a nonstick skillet, bring carrot and water to boil. Reduce heat; cover and simmer 5 minutes. Add broccoli, onion and zucchini; return to boil. Reduce heat; cover and simmer 2 minutes. Add salad dressing and oregano. Cook and stir over medium heat 4 minutes or until vegetables are tender and liquid is reduced.

Yield: 4 servings

FUN FACT – Oregano has a robust flavor: use sparingly. Popular in Mediterranean countries. It's often used in tomato sauce and on pizza. Also good in stews and sprinkled over fish and poultry.

Potato Tartlets

2½ pounds potatoes, cubed and peeled (peeling optional)
1 tablespoon butter or stick margarine
1 tablespoon grated onion
1 (8-ounce) cup reduced fat ricotta cheese
1 (8-ounce) cup reduced fat sour cream
1 teaspoon salt
1 teaspoon garlic powder
½ teaspoon dried rosemary
¼ teaspoon black pepper
2 egg whites
2 tablespoons dry bread crumbs
  Cooking spray

Preheat oven to 425 degrees.

In a large saucepan or pot cover potatoes with water and bring to a boil. Reduce heat and cook covered until potatoes are tender, about 20-25 minutes. Mash potatoes with butter or margarine and onion until small lumps of potatoes remain, do not over-mash.

In a mixing bowl, beat ricotta cheese, sour cream, salt, garlic powder, rosemary and black pepper until smooth. In a small bowl, beat egg whites until frothy and fold into cheese mixture. Fold egg white and cheese mixture into potatoes.

Generously coat 12 muffin cups with cooking spray and sprinkle an equal amount of bread crumbs into each muffin cup. Fill muffin cups with even amounts of potato mixture and smooth over tops. Bake uncovered until edges of potatoes are slightly browned, about 25-30 minutes. Cool on a rack for 15 minutes and loosen tartlets before inverting to remove.

Yield: 12 servings

153 calories, 6 grams fat (5 saturated), 20 grams carbohydrates, 2 grams fiber, 5 grams protein

ACTIVITY – <u>Youngstown</u> is home to the <u>Fort Niagara State Park</u> on Lake Ontario where year round recreation from soccer and boating to snowshoeing and cross-country skiing. (<u>Niagara</u>)

Green Beans with Walnuts

1½   pounds fresh green beans, cut
       into 2-inch pieces
½   cup coarsely chopped walnuts
2   tablespoons olive oil
1-2 garlic cloves, minced
½   teaspoon seasoned salt
¼   teaspoon pepper

Place beans in a large saucepan and cover with water. Bring to boil. Cook, uncovered, 8-10 minutes or until crisp-tender; drain. In a large skillet over medium heat, cook walnuts in oil 1-2 minutes or until lightly browned, stirring occasionally. Add beans, garlic, seasoned salt and pepper. Cook until heated through.

Yield: 8 servings

Sunny Snow Peas

½   cup orange juice
2   tablespoons honey
1   tablespoon butter or stick
       margarine
1-2 teaspoons grated orange peel
½   teaspoon salt
⅛   teaspoon ground cardamom
1   pound fresh snow peas or sugar
       snap peas

In a small saucepan, combine the first 6 ingredients; bring to boil. Reduce heat; simmer, uncovered, until mixture is reduced by half, about 15 minutes. In another saucepan, bring 1-inch water and peas to boil. Reduce heat; simmer, uncovered, for 5-6 minutes or until crisp-tender. Drain and place in a serving bowl. Pour sauce over peas and toss to coat.

Yield: 6 servings

FUN FACT – Did you know that butter is one of our oldest foods?

Sweet Potato Apple Bake

2   pounds sweet potatoes (about 3 medium)
2   medium apples, peeled and cored
1   tablespoon lemon juice
½   cup packed brown sugar
¼   cup chopped pecans
½   teaspoon ground cinnamon
½   teaspoon pumpkin pie spice
½   teaspoon orange extract
2   tablespoons butter or stick margarine

Place sweet potatoes in a saucepan and cover with water. Bring to boil; cook 20-25 minutes or until tender. Drain and cool. Peel potatoes and cut into ¼-inch slices. Place in a 13 x 9 x 2-inch baking dish coated with nonstick cooking spray.

Cut apples into ¼-inch rings; cut in half. Arrange over sweet potatoes. Sprinkle with lemon juice. Combine brown sugar, pecans, cinnamon, pumpkin pie spice and orange extract; sprinkle over apples. Dot with butter. Bake, uncovered at 350 degrees for 25-30 minutes or until apples are tender.

Yield: 7 servings

ACTIVITY – Wilson Tuscarora State Park, Wilson (Niagara) – This 396 acre park includes mature woods, open meadows and marshland with a variety of wildlife and plant life. Visitors can enjoy swimming, fishing, boating, hiking, skiing and snowmobiling.

Lemon-Maple Butternut Squash

1	large butternut squash (2½ pounds), halved lengthwise and seeded
¼	cup water
¼	cup maple syrup
1	tablespoon butter or stick margarine, melted
1	tablespoon lemon juice
½	teaspoon grated lemon peel

Place squash cut side down in an ungreased 13 x 9 x 2-inch baking dish. Add water. Cover and bake at 350 degrees for 50-60 minutes or until tender. Scoop out squash and place in a mixing bowl. Add syrup, butter, lemon juice and peel; beat until smooth.

Yield: 4 servings

Twice-Baked Potatoes

6	large baking potatoes
2	tablespoons butter or stick margarine, softened
1	cup 1% milk
¼	pound turkey bacon (about 9 slices), diced and cooked
1½	cups (6-ounce) shredded reduced-fat Cheddar cheese, divided
2	tablespoons minced chives
½	teaspoon salt
	Dash pepper

Bake potatoes at 375 degrees for 1 hour or until tender. Cool. Cut a thin slice off the top of each potato and discard. Scoop out pulp, leaving a thin shell. In a bowl, mash the pulp with butter. Stir in milk, bacon, 1 cup of cheese, chives, salt and pepper. Spoon into the potato shells.

Place on an ungreased cookie sheet. Bake at 375 degrees for 25-30 minutes or until heated through. Sprinkle with remaining cheese. Bake 2 minutes longer or until cheese is melted.

Yield: 6 servings

FUN FACT – There are twelve different types of squash, they are: acorn, buttercup, butternut, carnival, delicate, golden nugget, hubbard, kabocha, red kuri, spaghetti, sweet dumpling, and turban.

Cranberry Beets

6	cups sliced peeled fresh beets
1	(16-ounce) can whole-berry cranberry sauce
2	tablespoons orange juice
1	teaspoon grated orange peel
½	teaspoon salt

Place beets in a saucepan and cover with water; bring to boil. Reduce heat; cover and simmer 10 minutes or until tender. In another saucepan, heat cranberry sauce over medium heat until melted. Add orange juice, orange peel and salt. Drain beets; gently stir into cranberry mixture. Heat through.

Yield: 8 servings

Candied Carrots

4	cups sliced carrots
3	tablespoons reduced-calorie pancake syrup
1	tablespoon lemon juice
2	teaspoons minced fresh parsley
1	teaspoon butter or stick margarine
½	teaspoon salt
	Dash pepper

In a saucepan, place 1-inch of water and carrots. Bring to boil. Reduce heat; cover and simmer until crisp-tender. Drain. Stir in remaining ingredients. Simmer, uncovered, until most of the liquid has evaporated.

Yield: 6 servings

ACTIVITY – The Kavinosky Theater is located at D'Youville College in Buffalo (Erie).

Chocolate Soufflés

7   teaspoons sugar
⅓   cup sugar
½   cup packed brown sugar
⅓   cup cake flour
½   cup baking cocoa
2   teaspoons instant coffee granules
      or espresso powder
¾   cup water
4   ounces semi-sweet chocolate,
      chopped
3   egg yolks beaten
6   egg whites, room temperature
½   teaspoon cream of tartar
⅓   cup sugar
1   teaspoon powdered sugar

Preheat oven to 325 degrees. Spray seven 10-ounce ramekins with nonstick cooking spray. Coat the bottom and sides with 1 teaspoon sugar each.

In a saucepan combine ⅓ cup sugar, brown sugar, flour, cocoa and coffee. Stir in water until blended; bring to a boil and stir for 1 minute (mixture will be thick).

Remove from heat and stir in chocolate until melted. Remove a small amount of the mixture and stir into egg yolks. Return mixture with egg yolks to pan and stir constantly until mixed. Cool to room temperature.

In large bowl beat egg whites until foamy. Add cream of tartar and beat on medium speed until soft peaks form. Gradually add remaining ⅓ cup sugar, 1 tablespoon at a time, beating until stiff peaks form. Gently fold ¼ of the egg white mixture into the chocolate mixture. Fold in remaining egg white mixture.

Spoon batter into prepared ramekins and bake at 325 degrees until toothpick inserted in the center comes out clean.

Place on wire racks and dust with powdered sugar once cooled.

313 calories, 8 grams fat (4 saturated), 58 grams carbohydrates, 5 grams fiber, 7 grams protein

FUN FACT – Lemons contain more sugar than strawberries.

Traditional New York Style Cheesecake

Crust

½   cup (5-ounce) finely ground graham crackers or cookies such as chocolate or vanilla wafers or gingersnaps
5   tablespoons unsalted butter, melted
⅓   cup sugar
⅛   teaspoon salt

Cheesecake

5   (8-ounce) packages cream cheese, softened
1¾ cups sugar
3   tablespoons all-purpose flour
    Finely grated zest of 1 orange
    Finely grated zest of 1 lemon
5   large eggs
2   large egg yolks
½   teaspoon vanilla

For Crust: Stir together all crust ingredients and press onto bottom and 1-inch up the side of a buttered 9-inch springform pan. Fill right away or chill up to 2 hours.

For Cheesecake: Preheat oven to 450 degrees.

Beat together cream cheese, sugar, flour, and zests with an electric mixer until smooth. Add eggs and yolks, 1 at a time, then vanilla, beating on low speed until each ingredient is incorporated. Scrape down bowl between additions.

Put springform pan with crust in a shallow baking pan. Pour filling into crust (springform pan will be completely full) and bake in baking pan (to catch drips) in middle of oven 12 minutes, or until puffed. Reduce temperature to 200 degrees and continue baking until cake is mostly firm (center will still be slightly wobbly when pan is gently shaken), about 1 hour more.

Run a knife around top edge of cake to loosen and cool completely in springform pan on a rack. Chill cake, loosely covered, at least 6 hours. Remove side of pan and transfer cake to a plate. Bring to room temperature before serving.

Cheesecake keeps covered and chilled, 2 weeks.

Yield: 8-10 servings

ACTIVITY – The Dart Airport Aviation Museum in Mayville is a fun place to try a glider or airplane ride or even sign up for flight instruction. The museum includes a variety of aviation memorabilia.

Quick and Easy Fudge Brownies

2   sticks butter, softened
2   cups sugar
2   teaspoons vanilla
4   eggs
3   ounces unsweetened chocolate,
        melted
1   cup flour
1   cup chopped nuts, pecans or
        walnuts

Preheat oven to 325 degrees. Cream together butter, sugar and vanilla. Beat in eggs. Blend in chocolate. Add flour and nuts and stir until just combined.

Spread the batter into a greased 9 x 12-inch pan. Bake for 25-30 minutes.

FUN FACT – Ice Cream Is Chinese Food! When the famous explorer Marco Polo returned to his homeland of Italy, from China in 1295, he brought back a recipe. The recipe, was a Chinese recipe for a desert called "Milk Ice". However, Europeans substituted cream for the milk. Ice cream has been a hit ever since!

Chocolate Orange Turnovers

1½ ounces fine quality bittersweet chocolate (not unsweetened)
½ teaspoon freshly grated orange zest
1 large egg
1 thawed puff pastry sheet (from a 17¼ ounce package of frozen puff pastry sheets)
2 teaspoons sugar

Preheat oven to 425 degrees and lightly butter a baking sheet.

Chop chocolate and in a small bowl stir together with zest. In another small bowl lightly beat egg. Trim any uneven edges from pastry sheet and cut into 4 squares. Brush edges of pastry squares with some egg. Put ¼ chocolate mixture on center of each pastry square and fold each square diagonally in half, forming triangles. Seal edges by gently pressing together and crimp decoratively.

Brush tops of turnovers with egg and sprinkle with sugar. With a sharp knife cut a small steam vent in top of each turnover. On baking sheet bake turnovers in middle of oven until golden, about 12 minutes. Cool turnovers slightly on a rack. Serve turnovers warm.

Yield: 4 turnovers

ACTIVITY – Lily Dale Assembly, (Chautauqua) – a large spiritual community, offers clairvoyance and healing services. Overnight accommodations are available.

Make Ahead Peanut Butter Cookies

Make Ahead Cookie Mix

1½	cups butter
1	tablespoon salt
2	teaspoons baking powder
6	cups all-purpose flour

Combine first 3 ingredients well. Add flour slowly. Mix can be stored in a refrigerator for up to 4 weeks.

2	cups Make Ahead Cookie Mix
1	cup packed brown sugar
⅓	cup shortening
½	cup peanut butter
½	teaspoon vanilla extract
1	egg

Preheat oven to 375 degrees.

Combine 2 cups of Make Ahead Cookie Mix with brown sugar, shortening, peanut butter, vanilla, and egg.

Shape dough into balls. Place dough on ungreased cookie sheets. Flatten with a fork. Bake 7-11 minutes.

Yield: 12 servings

FUN FACT – Fortune cookies were invented in 1916 by George Jung, a Los Angeles noodle maker.

Thin, Crispy Chocolate Chip Cookies

1½   cups (7½-ounce) unbleached
      all-purpose flour
¼   teaspoon salt
¾   teaspoon baking soda
8   tablespoons (1 stick) unsalted
      butter, melted and cooled
½   cup granulated sugar
⅓   cup packed light brown sugar
3   tablespoons light corn syrup
1   large egg yolk
2   tablespoons milk
1   tablespoon vanilla extract
¾   cup (about 4½-ounces) semi-sweet
      chocolate chips

Adjust oven rack to middle position and heat oven to 375 degrees. Line 2 baking sheets with parchment paper; set aside. Sift flour, salt, and baking soda onto large sheet of parchment paper; set aside.

In bowl of standing mixer fitted with paddle attachment, beat melted butter, granulated sugar, brown sugar, and corn syrup at low speed until thoroughly blended, about 1 minute. Add yolk, milk, and vanilla; mix until fully incorporated and smooth, about 1 minute, scraping bottom and sides of bowl with rubber spatula as necessary. With mixer running on low speed, fold up 3 edges of parchment around dry ingredients to form a pouch and slowly shake dry ingredients into bowl; mix on low speed until just combined, about 2 minutes. Do not over-beat. Add chips and mix on low speed until distributed evenly throughout batter, about 5 seconds.

Leaving about 2-inches between each ball, scoop dough onto parchment-lined baking sheets with 1¼-inch (1 tablespoon capacity) ice cream scoop. Bake 1 sheet at a time, until cookies are deep golden brown and flat, about 12 minutes.

Cool cookies on baking sheet 3 minutes. Using wide metal spatula, transfer cookies to wire rack and let sit until crisped and cooled to room temperature. (Can be stored in airtight container for up to 1 week.)

Yield: About 4 dozen 2-inch cookies

ACTIVITY – Schoellkopf Geological Museum (Niagara) – located one-half mile down river from the American Falls. This museum offers a look into the formation of this natural wonder.

Coffee Pecan Loaf

2	cups flour
2½	teaspoons baking powder
½	teaspoon salt
⅔	cup shortening
1	cup sugar
2	tablespoons instant coffee
3	eggs
⅔	cup milk
1	teaspoon vanilla
1	cup chopped pecans or walnuts

Sift the flour, baking powder and salt into a bowl. In a second bowl, cream the shortening with sugar and instant coffee. Beat in eggs until light and fluffy. Add flour mixture alternately with the milk and vanilla. Add nuts. Spoon into greased loaf pan (or two small pans), bake 55 minutes at 350 degrees or until cake tester in the center comes out clean.

ACTIVITY – <u>Stull Observatory, Alfred University (Allegany)</u> – contains a unique combination of instruments to view our atmosphere. They house seven telescopes ranging in size from 8-32 inches.

Lite and Luscious Tiramisu

½ cup ground coffee beans
1¾ cups cold water
¼ cup Kahlúa (coffee-flavored liqueur), divided
½ cup mascarpone cheese
1 (8-ounce) package fat-free cream cheese, softened
⅓ cup packed brown sugar
¼ cup granulated sugar
2 (3-ounce) packages ladyfingers
2 teaspoons unsweetened cocoa, divided

Using ground coffee beans and cold water brew 1½ cups coffee and combine with Kahlúa in a shallow dish, cool.

Combine cheeses in a large bowl and beat at high speed until smooth. Add 2 tablespoons Kahlúa and sugars, beat until well blended. Split ladyfingers in half lengthwise. Quickly dip 24 ladyfinger halves, flat sides down, into coffee mixture. Place halves, dipped sides down, in the bottom of an 8-inch square baking dish (halves will be slightly overlapping). Spread half of cheese mixture over ladyfingers and sprinkle with 1 teaspoon cocoa. Repeat with remaining ladyfinger halves, coffee mixture, cheese mixture, and 1 teaspoon cocoa.

Place 1 toothpick in each corner of dish and 1 in the center of tiramisu (to prevent the plastic wrap from sticking to cheese mixture); cover with plastic wrap.

Chill for 2 hours.

Calories 134 (30% from fat); fat 4.5g (sat 2.2g, mono 1.5g, poly 0.4g); protein 3.3g; carb 21.7g.

ACTIVITY – The 1818 McClug Mansion and Chautauqua County Historical Society has Civil War and Native American artifacts, agricultural and craftsmen tools, a research library and a changing pictorial gallery.

Bread Pudding with Bourbon Sauce

Soufflés

1½   tablespoons raisins
½   cup sugar, plus more for
        sprinkling
        Scant ¼ teaspoon cinnamon
        Pinch of freshly grated nutmeg
1   large egg, lightly beaten
½   cup heavy cream
½   teaspoon pure vanilla extract
2   cups day old crustless French,
        Italian or challah bread cubes
        (½-inch)
3   large egg whites
        Pinch of cream of tartar

Bourbon Sauce

½   cup heavy cream
¾   teaspoon cornstarch dissolved in
        1 tablespoon water
1½   tablespoons sugar
1½   tablespoons bourbon

For Soufflé: Preheat the oven to 350 degrees. Butter an 8 x 4-inch loaf pan. Sprinkle the raisins on the bottom. In a bowl, combine ¼ cup of the sugar, the cinnamon and nutmeg. Whisk in the egg, cream and vanilla. Add the bread. Let stand for 5 minutes, stirring occasionally, until the liquid is absorbed.

Spoon the bread into the prepared loaf pan and smooth the top. Bake for 25 minutes, or until golden and set. Let cool slightly, then turn the bread pudding out onto a cutting board and coarsely chop it.

Butter a 3 cup ramekin or soufflé dish and sprinkle it with sugar, tapping out any excess. In a clean bowl, using an electric mixer beat the egg whites with the cream of tartar until frothy. Increase the speed to high and beat until soft peaks form. Gradually add the remaining ¼ cup of sugar and beat until stiff and glossy. Put half of the bread pudding in a medium bowl. Fold in ¼ of the beaten egg whites until just combined. Spoon the mixture into the ramekin. Add the remaining bread pudding to the bowl and fold in the remaining egg whites. Spoon the mixture into the ramekin, mounding it about 1-inch above the rim. Bake the soufflé for 25 minutes, or until golden and puffed.

Meanwhile, make the Bourbon Sauce: In a small saucepan, bring the cream to a boil. Whisk in the dissolved cornstarch and cook until slightly thickened, about 1 minute. Off the heat, add the sugar and bourbon. Return to the heat and simmer over moderately low heat for 1 minute.

As soon as the soufflé is done, poke a hole in the center and pour in half of the bourbon sauce. Serve the soufflé at once, passing the extra sauce on the side.

The bread pudding base and bourbon sauce can be refrigerated overnight. Bring both to room temperature before proceeding with the recipe.

Yield: 2 servings

FUN FACT – To determine the percentage of alcohol in a bottle of liquor divide the proof by two.

Dutch Orange Kugel

½ cup currants
1⅓ cups sour cream
1⅓ cups cottage cheese
3 large eggs
½ cup sugar
5 tablespoons unsalted butter, melted
1 tablespoon freshly grated orange zest
1 teaspoon vanilla
½ teaspoon cinnamon
¼ teaspoon salt
½ pound wide egg noodles
1 large Granny Smith apple
⅓ cup sliced blanched almonds

In a small bowl soak currants in hot water to cover 5 minutes and drain well.

In a blender blend together sour cream, cottage cheese, eggs, ¼ cup plus 2 tablespoons sugar, 3 tablespoons butter, zest, vanilla, ¼ teaspoon cinnamon, and salt until smooth.

Preheat oven to 350 degrees. Add butter a 2-quart gratin dish or other shallow baking dish.

In a kettle of salted boiling water cook noodles until just tender, about 5 minutes, and drain well. Peel apple and grate coarse into a bowl. Add noodles and toss with sour cream mixture and currants. Transfer mixture to prepared dish.

In a small bowl stir together remaining 2 tablespoons sugar, remaining ¼ teaspoon cinnamon, and almonds and sprinkle evenly over kugel. Drizzle top with remaining 2 tablespoons melted butter.

Bake kugel in middle of oven 40-45 minutes, or until cooked through and golden.

Yield: 6-8 servings as a side dish or dessert.

FUN FACT – A cow gives nearly 200,000 glasses of milk in her lifetime.

Index

a

B

T

V

W

Y

Z

☀️ Living Well in Western New York

Health For All Of Western New York
2495 Main Street, Suite 310
Buffalo, New York 14214
PHONE: 716.837.8400 • FAX: 716.837.8300
www.healthforall.org

Please send me:

Living Well in Western New York	@ $24.95 each	Quantity _____	$ _____
Shipping and handling	@ $ 4.95 each		$ _____
Sales tax *(NY residents only add 8%)*	@ $ 1.99 each		$ _____
		TOTAL ENCLOSED	$ _____

Ship to:

Name _____

Address _____

City _____ State _____ Zip Code _____

Make checks payable to Health For All Of Western New York

Charge to: (circle one)   Visa   MasterCard   Discover

Signature _____

Account Number _____ Expiration Date _____

- -

☀️ Living Well in Western New York

Health For All Of Western New York
2495 Main Street, Suite 310
Buffalo, New York 14214
PHONE: 716.837.8400 • FAX: 716.837.8300
www.healthforall.org

Please send me:

Living Well in Western New York	@ $24.95 each	Quantity _____	$ _____
Shipping and handling	@ $ 4.95 each		$ _____
Sales tax *(NY residents only add 8%)*	@ $ 1.99 each		$ _____
		TOTAL ENCLOSED	$ _____

Ship to:

Name _____

Address _____

City _____ State _____ Zip Code _____

Make checks payable to Health For All Of Western New York

Charge to: (circle one)   Visa   MasterCard   Discover

Signature _____

Account Number _____ Expiration Date _____

Living Well in Western New York

A Four Season Recipe Book & Activites Guide

Living Well in Western New York

2495 Main Street, Suite 310
Buffalo, New York 14214
PHONE: 716.837.8400 • FAX: 716.837.8300
www.healthforall.org

Copyright © 2004

First Printing   December 2004

ISBN: 0-9762665-0-4

WIMMER
COOKBOOKS

A CONSOLIDATED GRAPHICS COMPANY

800.548.2537   wimmerco.com